HOW TO DO EVERYTHING

Your Guide to Life Hacks, Cooking, Money, Health, Technology, Survival Skills, Career Planning, and More!

JAMIE MYERS

ISBN: 978-1-957590-48-6

For questions, email: Support@AwesomeReads.org

Please consider writing a review!

Just visit: AwesomeReads.org/review

FREE BONUS

SCAN TO GET OUR NEXT BOOK FOR FREE!

TABLE OF CONTENTS

INTRODUCTION

Current research suggests that, although adults seek higher education, many still experience a "life skills gap" that causes unnecessary stress, strain, and struggle. While schools once taught life skills in classes like home economics, today's schools focus more on academic education and less on personal skills like housekeeping, financial planning, and wellness. Even the most well-educated people may never have learned about 401Ks, taxes, organization, cooking, or countless other tasks that have a monumental impact on overall success.

Even if you know these basic skills, you may feel like you're barely coping — throwing together meals without any real understanding of cooking techniques or choosing random cleaning products because you aren't sure which is the "right" one. Organizing your life can seem impossible when juggling a career, social life, and any other responsibilities you may have. However, when you take time to learn the fundamental skills of life, you build a stronger foundation for your life and thrive — instead of just survive.

EXPLORING A RANGE OF SKILLS

This book was created for people with varying levels of knowledge; no matter where you're starting, you can get to where you want to be and learn any skills you lack. From everyday life hacks to personal growth skills, you'll learn how to rise to the occasion and clear any obstacle that stands in your way.

Each chapter starts with the basics, then expands on those basics to help you really develop those skills. Thus, you're encouraged to go beyond your bare minimum needs and explore what parts of each topic give you the most satisfaction, helping you find peace and balance in your life.

LIVING A FULLER, HAPPIER, & HEALTHIER LIFE

As we mentioned, the goal is to do more than just survive—you want to thrive and use your resources wisely to keep building on your achievements. You want to spend less time worrying or wondering what you should do and, instead, act with confidence in all areas of your life.

This book isn't just an instruction manual on how to do things; it will give you tools to deal with any difficulties in your path. Thus, while there's some instructional material, the focus is on giving you all the information you need to make smart decisions and solve problems before they get worse. There's no "one-size-fits-all" approach to life; most of the time, there's more than one effective way to tackle the same task.

Some of the topics discussed in this book may seem mundane; However, when you develop competency in these areas, they become less boring and can even give you a sense of control over your life. You'll learn to be more efficient with these tasks, and in some areas, you may even find a passion for what was once a chore. There will always be things you have to do but don't like, but those with the most satisfactory lives know that both attitude and approach make a profound difference in how you feel about even the tasks you hate most.

HOW TO USE
THIS BOOK

If you encounter skills in this book that you already know or have no desire to work on, there's nothing wrong with skipping around based on your interests and needs. However, we urge you to at least browse each chapter, even if you already have a basic understanding of the subject area. Growth opportunities often come where you least expect them.

While you can read this book in its entirety before taking action, it might work better to slow down and test out an individual chapter before moving on. It's up to you how you want to integrate the skills into your life. Remember, you can always revisit a chapter for a refresher or inspiration.

CHAPTER ONE: EVERYDAY LIFE HACKS

If you've ever looked around you and thought your life was a complete mess, you're not alone. While trying to balance work, family, friends, and everything else, the "everything else" can sometimes devolve into chaos — either because you can't seem to find time, or you're too overwhelmed. The solution is to implement a few everyday life hacks, which can have a big impact with relatively little effort. These life hacks are powerful because they'll save you time in the long run, allowing you to dedicate more time to what you love most without feeling like your life is falling apart.

ORGANIZING YOUR SCHEDULE

When you have a million things to do, creating a schedule is a must if you want to get things done. The first step to organizing your schedule is to know your priorities. Think about what activities are the most important; knowing what matters the most gives you a better grasp of how to organize your schedule.

Once you've established your priorities, start by allocating time to your highest priorities, then work down the list. Begin by focusing on items that have established time commitments or are of the highest importance. For instance, many people start with their work hours and go from there because they spend a significant amount of their time at work.

When creating your schedule, it's important to leave some wiggle room. An overly-rigid schedule is hard to adapt if — well, when — something unexpected comes up. However, when you leave some room for the "what-ifs," you have the flexibility to adjust as needed.

Keep in mind that not every day needs to be perfectly balanced. One day, you may focus on work, while another, you focus more on family. You don't have to divide everything equally each day; rather, find a balance that works best for the ebb and flow of your life.

QUICK CLEANING TIPS FOR A TIDY HOME

You may be surprised to hear that you don't have to devote an entire day to cleaning if you want to keep things neat. While that's certainly one method, it's more efficient to do a little cleaning each day. When you perform separate tasks on different days, they become more manageable, and it's easier to keep up without feeling like you're constantly falling behind.

To start a cleaning routine, create a weekly schedule, assigning tasks to complete each day. Honestly, you don't even need to be that regimented about the tasks if it's too strict for you. Instead, keep a list of tasks to do each week, then devote a certain amount of time each day to cleaning. Then, you can choose which task you want to work on each day until each is checked off the list. If you live with roommates or family, be sure to divide tasks fairly. This won't always mean a fifty-fifty split, though; instead, focus on working together to maintain your shared environment.

MAXIMIZING STORAGE SPACE IN SMALL SPACES

When you want to add more space, look at your furniture first; multi-functional furniture can do double duty. For example, storage ottomans are a great place to stow away extra stuff. Additionally, vertical storage is an effective way to add more storage to a room without making it feel cluttered. With this type of storage, you can organize more effectively by putting your most-used items lower and less-frequently used items higher.

As for your closets, having only a rod to hang clothing on severely limits your options. Add shelving units or cabinets to expand your space. Don't neglect any available floor or wall space in your closets.

Don't forget to look down! Underneath your bed is a great place to put items you can stow away when they're not in use without compromising the overall look of your space.

Make sure you have a system in place; don't just shove things in a drawer or a bin. Organize items in designated spots so you can fit more in the space and to know where your items are.

When you're looking to create effective small spaces, don't be afraid to get creative! If you think a certain organizational system might work better, give it a try, and experiment with moving your furniture and decor to make each item work better for your space. It'll take some work to find the perfect combination, but it's well worth the effort.

SIMPLIFYING MEAL PLANNING AND PREPARATION

At the start of each week, take time to plan your meals and get the supplies you need. If you live with other people, this process may also include assigning tasks, so each person knows what they're responsible for providing or preparing.

Once you have a plan, prepare the portions you'll use over the week. Cutting vegetables is a great way to use meal planning to your advantage. This way, after a busy day, you can simply throw things together without having to dirty tons of dishes and do the most tedious work. Save time by doing tasks all at once. For instance, if you want to eat bell pepper strips for snacks all week, it's much harder to cut the pepper each time than prepare portions for the entire week.

When you prep your meals, you also tend to make healthier choices; reducing the effort that goes into eating when you're tired keeps you from reaching for less nutritious options. Prepare as much as you can when you're feeling motivated and spare yourself effort when you have less energy.

EASY FIXES FOR COMMON PROBLEMS

When it comes to running a household, there's no doubt that difficulties will arise. Even small snags can feel overwhelming if you don't know where to start. Fortunately, preparing for common scenarios makes problem solving easy.

Some of the most common household repairs include unclogging sinks and drains, dealing with squeaky hinges and leaks, and patching up walls. This section offers an overview of fixing basic household issues, but you'll learn more detailed methods throughout this book.

The Most Common Tools

If you want to fix issues yourself, keeping a stocked toolbox ensures you are prepared to handle small repairs and projects as they arise.

Some common tools include:

- Claw hammer
- A set of screwdrivers of various sizes (both flat-head and Phillips-head)
- Pliers
- Adjustable wrenches
- Nails of various sizes
- Level
- Tape measure
- Utility knife
- Putty knife
- Ruler or yardstick
- Flashlight
- File
- Personal protective gear (gloves, glasses, hearing protection)
- Power drill and drill bits
- Clamps

This list includes some of the most versatile and essential tools for basic needs. You don't have to get these all at once, but a collection of tools allows you to take on more fix-it projects. You also want to have a designated place to store your tools and keep them organized.

Address Issues Right Away

When an issue in your household needs attention, it can be tempting to procrastinate, hoping that by ignoring the problem, it'll just go away. However, if you address it right away, the issue is less likely to become a bigger problem that requires an expensive solution.

If It Seems Too Easy, It Probably Is

It's human nature to want easy fixes; when we have a problem, we want it handled as soon as possible. However, taking shortcuts can often lead to a long-term hassle. If you let the core issue fester, eventually it will require proper attention. Often, this leads to more work and more expenses. So, save yourself the trouble by doing it right the first time.

When in Doubt, Call an Expert

DIY fixes are a great way to take care of your household and save money, but it's important to know your limits. If you don't have the knowledge or skill to fix a problem, you might end up making it worse. In these cases, it's best to call an expert. At the very least, do some serious research before diving into a fix-it project.

CHAPTER TWO: BASIC COOKING SKILLS

We need to eat to live, but that doesn't mean we're eating well — and when we're not eating well, we're probably not living that well either. Meals aren't just about physical nourishment, but also mental nourishment. It's no wonder that the word "companion" stems from the Latin words com (with) and panis (bread), highlighting the profound role meals have in our lives.

Meals allow us to connect, share, and enjoy some downtime with ourselves and others. Everyone has meals that remind them of their family, traditions, and culture. By learning basic cooking skills, you both provide for and connect with yourself.

It's okay to eat convenience meals and grab-and-go foods from time to time, but when you do it all the time, it's easy to miss out on nutrients provided by eating a variety of foods. Plus, by learning to make a few simple recipes, you can customize your meals while saving money on expensive takeout and convenience foods.

BOILING WATER: THE FOUNDATION OF COOKING

It's common to hear that someone is "such a bad cook that they can't even boil water!" The truth is that most people know that placing a pot of water over heat will eventually result in big, lively bubbles as the temperature reaches 212 degrees Fahrenheit (slightly less at higher elevations.)

Of course, that doesn't mean there are no lessons to learn about boiling water! Learning the ideal method for boiling water will save you time and fuss. By boiling water, you can prepare recipes involving pasta, vegetable, and grains in no time.

Before you start, think about what you want. Make sure you have a big enough pot to hold the amount of water you need and what you want to cook. Some recipes don't specify the amount of water, but it's better to have too much than too little; as you are no doubt aware, water evaporates in the form of steam, and you can always drain some off.

The old saying goes that "a watched pot will never boil," but there are ways to speed the process up. Contrary to common myths, additives like baking soda or salt won't make water boil faster, but the amount of water and the type of container you use might. More water takes longer to boil, but depth also impacts the boiling time. The shallower the pot or pan is, the faster it will boil; this is because more water is touching the bottom of the pan, which is, of course, the hottest part. As you boil your water, pop on the lid to keep heat circulating.

You can also give your water a head start by using hot water from your tap. An electric kettle speeds the process up even more, as it's designed specifically to heat water fast. Some of these devices can even maintain a specific temperature, so the water is hot and ready whenever you want to use it.

While boiling water is one of the easiest things in the kitchen, it also reminds you of one of the hardest lessons for any inspiring cook: When you're in the kitchen, no skill goes as far as patience. Even with tips and tricks to optimize your time, sometimes, you just have to wait. The good news is that, while waiting for your water to boil, you can start preparing your other ingredients.

COOKING TERMS & MEASUREMENTS

Looking at a recipe might feel overwhelming if it contains measurements or instructions that you don't understand. While some recipes certainly aren't fit for beginners, most are designed with ordinary people in mind, so take a deep breath and dive in. After learning a few basic terms, you'll be able to follow just about any recipe.

Unpacking Common Measurements

Before we get into technique, you need to understand cooking measurements. These come in various forms, including volume, weight, and temperature. Which measurements you use depends on what you're making (and what the recipe says). Different countries may use different units of measurement than you're used to, but each can be converted easily, allowing you to use recipes from around the world.

The first measurement we'll cover is temperature. Temperature is commonly used for ovens, but other devices, like fryers and convection ovens, use temperature measurements. In the United States, temperature is measured in Fahrenheit, generally ranging from 200 to 500 degrees, while most other countries use Celsius, generally ranging from 95 to 260 degrees (°). Most recipes provide specific temperatures, but you can generally judge oven temperatures from low to very hot.

- Low: 200°-250° Fahrenheit (95°-120° Celsius)
- Medium: 300°-350° Fahrenheit (150°-175° Celsius)

- Medium-Hot: 350°-400° Fahrenheit (175°-200° Celsius)
- Hot: 400°-450° Fahrenheit (175°-200° Celsius)
- Very Hot: 450°-500° Fahrenheit (230°-260° Celsius)

One common way to measure both liquid and dry ingredients is in volume, often using measuring cups or spoons. Generally, you use separate measuring cups for liquid and dry ingredients; dry measures are designed to be filled to the top and leveled with a knife or spatula, while liquid ones leave a little space at the top. In a pinch, use whatever you have—most recipes aren't so specific that tiny differences will ruin the final product.

Some common volume measuring amounts you'll see include:

- Teaspoon (tsp, or sometimes a lowercase t)
- Tablespoon (tbs, tbsp, or capital T)
- Fluid ounce (fl. oz.—different from a regular ounce, which refers to weight)
- Cup (C)
- Quart (qt)
- Pint (pt)
- Gallon (Gal)
- Milliliter (mL)

Some recipes include weighted measurements, designed to be measured with a food scale. Weight is used in recipes that require extra precision, but it's more common in European countries. Weight is also used to measure meat and veggies since that's how these foods are commonly sold.

Examples of weighted measurements include:

- Grams (g)

- Ounces (oz)
- Kilograms (kg)

Most measurements can be converted to another form; for instance, one cup equals 16 tablespoons. You can also find conversion tables to adapt volume to weight (or vice versa.) In most cases, a basic set of measuring cups and spoons will suffice, but if you ever need help, online converters can help you do the math automatically.

MOIST HEAT COOKING

"Moist heat" refers to methods using liquid or steam to cook, including:

Boiling: Boiling food involves submerging it in water or another liquid at boiling point (212° F), which is easy to identify by a bubbling surface. Boiling is often used for ingredients like pasta and potatoes.

Simmering: A simmer is just below a liquid's boiling point (180°-205° F). When a liquid is at a simmer, you'll see small, rolling bubbles (less robust than at a boil.) Simmering is used for a range of recipes, including sauces, soups, and veggies.

Steaming: To steam ingredients, you'll use a steamer basket above the boiling water rather than submerging them in the liquid. Steaming is most often used for veggies and fish because it cooks, while retaining nutrients.

Poaching: Poaching involves cooking food in liquid at a lower temperature (140°-180° F), when the liquid ripples but does not yet bubble. It's often used for fish and eggs because these foods can be easily torn by boiling.

Blanching: Blanching is often used for veggies, to retain a vibrant color and crispness. When blanching, the food is dipped in boiling water for a short time, then put into an ice bath. Generally, actual cooking time is between one to five minutes.

Ice bath: While not technically a moist heat cooking method, for some recipes, you may use an ice bath to stop the cooking process right away (as with blanching).

DRY HEAT TECHNIQUES

"Dry heat" methods are used in a variety of settings, but the most common are a stove or oven. As the name implies, dry heat relies on food having direct contact with cooking equipment, rather than using liquid.

Bake: Baking occurs in an oven or convection oven, using hot air to cook your food at an even rate. The term "roasting" is often used when baking savory foods, while "baking" is more commonly used for sweets. However, these terms are somewhat interchangeable.

Broil: Broiling is a lot like baking, but usually at a higher heat, and generally only cooks one side of the item. Broiling is common when you want to get a nice brown crust, so it's good for casseroles or veggies. You must watch broiling items carefully, though, because they can burn quickly.

Sauté: This method involves cooking an item on the stove at high heat. Generally, some sort of oil is heated in the pan, and you'll periodically shake or move items with a spoon or spatula to get even heat.

Char: Charring means blackening an item to create a unique flavor. When using this method, be careful to remove charred items when you see them start to bubble to avoid burning.

Sear: When you sear or "brown" an item, you cook it in a pan, piece by piece, browning each side without stirring the pan's contents. This technique is often used for big pieces of meat.

Frying: Because of the properties of oil, frying is usually considered a dry heat method. You can "deep fry" an item, submerging it in oil, or you can "pan fry" an item, which is similar to sautéing but generally uses more oil. The amount of oil is usually specified in the recipe (often one inch or halfway up the item you're frying).

Braising

Braising combines both dry and moist cooking and is good for cuts of meat that tend to be tough. You'll start by browning the food, covering it with liquid, and cooking it for a longer time over low heat. You may sometimes see braising called "stewing."

ENCOUNTERING UNFAMILIAR TERMS

When trying different recipes, you may encounter unfamiliar or more complex terms; often this happens with recipes from different countries of origin. The important thing is that, when you see something unfamiliar, you don't panic!

Modern technology makes it easy to search the internet for any unfamiliar terms you may find. Many concepts will require practice, but don't be afraid to try them out. Do a little research, then dive into a new technique. Online videos are a great way to witness a technique, allowing you to imitate it with ease.

While recipes can seem like a foreign language at first, as you expose yourself to more of them, the terms will become normalized, and your skills will increase with practice.

KNIFE SKILLS

If you've ever seen a cooking show, you might watch in awe as the host chops, dices, and slices with unbelievable speed and precision. While you don't need to be a master chef to get by in the kitchen, having proper knife skills can make cooking more efficient and fun—not to mention safer. Now, it's time to get out your knife and sharpen those skills!

Purchasing a Quality Knife

Before you do anything else, make sure you have a good knife to work with. Chefs debate which brand or type is best, and each has their own preference, so there's no magic answer to which is best. However, there are some things to consider when choosing the right knives for you.

There are specific knives designed for each separate task in the kitchen. While it's possible to make do with whatever you have, it's best to have a set that includes a chef's knife, utility knife, paring knife, bread knife, carving knife, cleaver, slicing knife, boning knife, and filet knife. Santoku knives, originally from Japan, are also becoming more popular in Western kitchens for their finesse. Because the chef's knife is the most versatile of all the knives, getting a good chef's knife should be your top priority.

You want your knife to be sharp. Many people are nervous that sharp knives are more dangerous, but actually, dull knives are more likely to cause harm because dull knives require more pressure, reducing control. Dull knives also encourage poor knife habits that can increase your risk in the kitchen. Thus, to keep your knives sharp, invest in a sharpening stone or electric knife sharpener.

Good knives are often made from materials like stainless steel (most common, affordable, and easily sharpened), carbon steel (durable, but requires more care), Damascus steel (durable, flexible, and pricey), and ceramic (incredibly sharp, but not quite as durable and hard to sharpen—better for smaller knives). If you're interested in learning more advanced cooking skills, you may want to invest in higher-end materials; however, for most home cooks, stainless steel works well.

Using Your Knife

Pull out your cutting board (preferably one that grips well) and whatever you want cut. A proper grip improves your control of the knife, so grasp it firmly, but not tightly enough to impede your maneuverability. With your thumb and index finger, hold the base, or "bolster," of the blade, and wrap your other fingers around the handle.

It's important, of course, to protect your fingers. When holding the ingredient to be cut, make your fingers into a "claw" shape, tucking your fingers in so they're further from the knife than your knuckles. Stabilize either side of the ingredient with your thumb and pinky while your other three fingers grip the top of the item. It may feel strange at first, but as you practice, this position will become natural, allowing you to cut more safely and efficiently.

Not all foods will sit nice and flat for you. If you've ever cut a potato, onion, or anything else with rounded edges, you know that wobbly veggies can be a huge challenge. Your goal should always be to find stability, so cutting off the bottom or halving it to create a flat side is a good way to solve the problem.

Slicing

Slicing is a good place to start building a foundation for other cutting techniques. Begin by curling your hand into the proper cutting position. Then, move the knife up and down with a rocking motion, moving your clawed hand back as you cut.

You can judge the size of your slices by using the knuckle of your middle finger as a rough measurement of how wide each slice should be. If you're cutting something long and thin, you may want to use a bias slice, which you can accomplish by cutting the item diagonally.

Chopping

Chopping involves creating smaller pieces, and it's okay if they aren't perfectly uniform. If you have a food processor, you can use it to chop faster, but it's also good to know how to do it manually.

To chop manually, use the same rocking motion as slicing, combined with the claw hand, to chop your food into smaller pieces. You may need to cut lengthwise, then chop in the other direction, depending on the size you need the food to be. Whatever you're chopping, don't worry about perfection; focus on getting the hand position and rocking motion down.

Dicing

When you dice, you cut your food into cubes, which should be as uniform as possible. You may have to adjust a little based on what you're cutting, but generally, you'll want to cut the food into sticks the size of the cube you need. Putting your hand into the claw form will keep the sticks together as you cut them across into cubes. Dicing is as easy as that!

Onions are perhaps more challenging to dice because they require some extra techniques—and you may have to do so through tears—but you should always begin by cutting off the stem and slicing the onion in half (but keep the root attached.) From there, put the flat side down with the root facing away from you and begin making your lengthwise cuts, stopping just short of the root to keep the onion together.

Next, rotate the onion so the root is facing outward and make horizontal cuts (parallel to the cutting surface), again stopping just short of the root. Finally, make your last cuts, and the onion will fall into those nice little squares!

MASTERING BASIC COOKING TECHNIQUES

It's one thing to know what techniques like sautéing, roasting, and grilling are, but it's another thing to know how to do them well. While these methods can seem intimidating on a recipe card, they're straightforward and easy once you get the hang of them.

Sautéing

The key to sautéing is to cook food by making the food "jump" — in fact, the term comes from the French verb "sauter," meaning to jump. This process is great for browning foods. It's most often used for veggies, and it's a good way to add extra flavor to vegetables without having to put in a lot of effort.

Before you put any food in the pan, drizzle a small amount of oil in it. Each oil has its own smoke point, which means they all cook differently. Generally, the most common oils for sautéing have a lower smoke point and add distinct flavors. These include extra virgin olive oil, along with sesame, butter, and coconut oils. Safflower or canola oil can also be used, but they tend to have less flavor, so they're better reserved for roasting or frying.

Start by heating your pan over medium-high heat for about one minute. Each stove is different, and it can take a while to learn exactly how hot each setting on your stove gets since they don't generally include actual temperatures.

Once your pan is hot, add whatever fat or oil you're using. Each recipe requires a different amount, but usually, a tablespoon or two is sufficient. You don't want to add a ton of oil—you're sautéing, not frying! After the oil heats up, it's time to add the ingredients.

During the cooking process, stir or shake the ingredients regularly to ensure even cooking. If the oil starts to smoke, turn the stove down a little. Generally, it will take around five to eight minutes for veggies to sauté. However, some recipes may require veggies to be "al dente," so they'll come out firm but still tender when bitten into.

Roasting

This technique requires more time, but most of it doesn't require direct action, so you can do other things while your food cooks. Roasting is an indirect heating method usually used for larger cuts of meat, especially tough ones. Cooking at a lower temperature for a longer time helps the meat break down so it'll be tender. Veggies are commonly added to provide flavor and variety. Roasting allows you to cook an item evenly.

There are multiple ways to roast your food, such as a roasting oven, but you can use your normal oven. To get the effect of a roast in a faster timeframe, a pressure cooker is a great tool that keeps the meat moist, but it's certainly not necessary for good results.

Most recipes will give you clear instructions on how to roast specific meats, but here are a few tips for better results:

The process starts before you even get the meat in the oven. You'll need to let the oven preheat, of course, to ensure it's at the right temperature when you put your meat in. It also helps to take your meat out of the fridge, so it reaches room temperature before you put it in the oven.

When seasoning the meat, be liberal with salt and pepper to add flavor and help the overall cooking process. For increased juiciness, you can add butter or oil over the meat. When it's time to put it in the oven, place the meat on a roasting rack.

As it cooks, avoid opening the oven often, as this lets the hot air out, reducing the oven temperature. Only open the oven about thirty minutes before the recipe indicates to give it a quick check, and only as needed based on the roast's progress. Once the roast reaches temperature, take it out of the oven, cover the pan with foil, and let it rest for about fifteen minutes before serving.

Grilling

Grilling is often associated with barbeque grills, but you can also find indoor, smokeless grills to achieve a similar effect. Grilling is relatively simple and perfect for summertime. Different grills offer varied techniques, flavors, and overall grilling experiences, so it's a great way to have fun finding new ways of bringing flavor to existing dishes.

Before putting anything on your grill, consider which kind of grill you have, and make sure the grill is preheated. For a charcoal grill, you'll need crushed lump charcoal known as "briquettes." You can also add flavor with water-soaked wood chips. Gas grills are easier to start; they're powered by propane and only require you to turn the knob, just as you would a stove. This makes gas grills the most common type in the United States. However, the gas grill doesn't offer the same smoky flavor as charcoal, so many grill fanatics prefer charcoal.

Once your grill reaches the desired temperature, you can start cooking, using either direct or indirect heat. Indirect heat involves cooking over a part of the grill without coals or flames, while direct heat requires you to put the food over the coals or flames, usually on the grate. Covering the grill gives you a faster, more even cook, which is good if the meat is one inch or thicker.

For thinner foods, you can still cover the grill but be prepared for a speedy cook. Research how long it generally takes to get your meat to the desired temperature and use a thermometer to judge whether the meat is fully cooked.

Keep in mind that, as meat sits — even when it's removed from the grill — it will cook a little more, so some recipes will advise that you let your meat sit before eating. In other cases, it's best to eat meat straight from the grill to avoid overcooking. If you're cooking veggies or other non-protein items, you'll likely be able to visually tell when they're ready to remove from the grill.

COOKING DELICIOUS MEALS ON A BUDGET

Cooking can be expensive, especially when you need a lot of ingredients, but below, we've compiled some tips to make delicious meals on a budget.

- Look for discounted ingredients and build your meals around those ingredients.
- Use canned or frozen foods when needed, especially out-of-season fruits or vegetables. Dried grains or beans are also good options to save money.
- Choose fruits or vegetables that are in season; out-of-season produce is always more expensive. You can even go to a farmers' market, then bulk-freeze produce, or grow them yourself.
- Buying the whole meat (such as the whole chicken) or a larger cut and using it in multiple ways is another way to reduce costs.
- Try cooking vegetarian meals, which are often less expensive than meat dishes (and better for the environment!)
- Learn to make egg dishes. Eggs are one of the most affordable protein choices, and they're super versatile, too.
- Freeze leftovers to avoid wasting food. This also means you'll have ready-made meals when you're busy or haven't been shopping.
- Plan what you want to eat during the week. This allows you to buy only what you need and avoid wasting extras.
- Buy in bulk whenever you can, including spices, baking supplies, and dry goods. Just be careful not to buy more than you'll use.

CHAPTER THREE:
HOME MAINTENANCE
AND DIY REPAIRS

If you're a homeowner or even a renter, taking care of your home can take a fair bit of time. However, with a little bit of patience and basic DIY and maintenance skills, you can handle many emerging problems, saving yourself time, money, and stress.

CHANGING A LIGHTBULB

Changing a lightbulb certainly doesn't seem all that complex. After all, all you've got to do is unscrew one light and put in another, right? However, there are some things to consider to ensure you're safely and effectively swapping bulbs.

When changing a lightbulb, most people want to do it as quickly as possible, to the point that they forget to turn the power off. Going to the fuse box and switching off the fuse for the room where your light is ensures you don't get electrocuted. Most people just turn off the light switch, which generally works, but there's still a chance that a fixture can still have power connected. Old buildings and houses in certain areas don't always follow the best electrical practices, so the best way to be sure power is cut off is to start at your fuse box.

You also want to watch out for burns; while hotter incandescent bulbs have been banned in the United States, LED lightbulbs can still get quite hot, especially car bulbs. Thus, before removing a lightbulb, make sure it's had time to cool down.

Once you're sure the bulb has cooled, you can start changing it. If it's an overhead light or above your reach, don't even think about reaching for that rolling desk chair or rickety old stool! We've all been there—precariously perched on the nearest object—but it's not worth the risk. A solid step ladder is an ideal choice, and if you have small kids or pets around, make sure they don't accidentally knock you over.

With some light fixtures, it's easy just to reach up and unscrew the lightbulb, but if you have a dome over your light, you'll need to grip it with your palm and turn it counterclockwise, like opening a pill bottle. Some domes may be tricky to remove, so be patient. In some cases, you may even have to remove screws before twisting the dome free.

Most bulbs come out easily when you twist them counterclockwise, but if you're having trouble for whatever reason, take a deep breath. Be gentle with the bulb; you don't want it to shatter. With patience and continued effort, it should screw loose.

If the bulb does shatter, don't panic! You can use the potato method, cutting a raw potato in half, then pressing the potato into the bulb's base, enabling you to rotate the base and get the broken bulb off. Unfortunately, you won't be able to use the potato for dinner, but at least you won't cut your fingers trying to get a lightbulb out!

The act of screwing the new bulb into the socket is intuitive, but make sure you use the right wattage. Not all lights are created equal; a bulb that's too strong can create too much heat and even a fire, while a bulb that isn't strong enough might cause issues like premature breakage. However, generally, you can use a 5-10-watt LED bulb in your fixtures because most lights don't output maximum power anyway. The old bulb should have its voltage written at its base, and the fixture should also have voltage information somewhere on it, so double-check the wattage you need.

Once the new bulb is in, you can put the fixture back together, and all you have left to deal with is disposing of the old bulb. Most bulbs can be thrown away or recycled, but some have special disposal instructions. Incandescent, halogen, and LED bulbs don't have toxic elements, so they can be carefully thrown away like any other glass item.

However, compact fluorescent light (CFL), high-intensity discharge (HID), and fluorescent tubes require careful recycling to avoid hazards, so take extra steps to avoid breakage with these bulbs. Home improvement stores sometimes have recycling options, and an internet search can give you the exact recycling locations in your area.

FIXING A LEAKY FAUCET: PLUMBING 101

If you've ever heard that constant dripping from your sink, you know how quickly it can get annoying. Though those little drops can seem like nothing, when you get your water bill, you immediately see the difference a leaky appliance can make. Fortunately, there are many ways to deal with basic plumbing concerns.

First, be as gentle with your plumbing systems as possible to reduce wear and promote a longer lifespan. Accordingly, when dealing with plumbing issues, you want to start with manual methods, and only when those methods don't work should you turn to chemicals. Using chemicals prematurely can do damage, especially if you use them for unclogging drains (more on that in the next section.)

Common issues you'll encounter include leaky faucets and running toilets. These problems can cost you a lot of money and be a general nuisance. When a faucet leaks, start by turning off the water supply valves, which you'll find beneath the sink. You can then take apart the handle of the faucet. Often, all you'll have to do is replace O-rings or washers, which wear out over time. For toilets, the problem is often the flapper valve, which is connected to a chain inside the toilet. New valves are relatively easy to install using the provided instructions.

Your at-home plumbing should also include maintenance. Take care of your water heater to make it last longer. Most water heaters last eight to twelve years, but you can prolong their lives by draining sediment in the tank. As part of the maintenance process, you should also monitor your water heat, as temperature changes may indicate an issue. Water pressure changes are also a sign to investigate further.

Solving these issues can seem overwhelming if you haven't dealt with them before, but videos can offer tips to correct problems with minimal stress. However, if you think you might make something worse if you try to fix it yourself, you should probably call a plumber.

EASY SOLUTIONS FOR (MORE) PLUMBING ISSUES

One of the most dreaded household issues is a clogged drain, which can occur when soap scum, debris, or hair builds up. Drain clogs are bound to happen, and it's pretty inconvenient to wait for a plumber every time. Sooner or later, you'll have a clog; no matter how fancy, all drain systems eventually collect debris. The good news is that you can deal with most drain clogs on your own.

Set aside the liquid-draining cleaner for now — if all goes well, you won't even need it! Start with tools like a plunger or drain snake to try to clear the debris from the drain. You want to evaluate the situation and start to consider what tools you have handy and where you want to start.

When using a plunger, you don't want to be violent. Instead, create suction by making sure the plunger seals around the area. Exert force gradually, then firmly pull back. The suction allows you to use gravity in your favor, so you should feel some tension with the plunger against the surface. When plunging a sink, it helps to cover the overflow hole, as this ensures the pressure is being adequately leveraged. The same basic concept applies to bathtub drains as well.

If a plunger doesn't work, you can turn to a drain snake. Feed the snake into the drain, cranking the handle as you go. Continue to advance the wire as needed, gradually progressing through the pipe. You can break the clog and bring it up the pipe. For tubs, you can feed the snake through the overflow opening, which generally gives you a straight shot. Using the drain itself can be challenging in tubs because the T-shape is tricky to navigate.

Sometimes, you may want to use chemical tools, but these don't generally eliminate stoppages. They can be used for some slow drains in selective circumstances, though. Baking soda and vinegar are good options for slow drains, and they aren't as abrasive as store-bought drain cleaners. Chemical drain cleaners may help with slow drains, but should be used sparingly, as they can eat away pipes and cause tons of issues in the future. Pour chemicals in gradually, following the instructions on the bottle. Be patient and allow products time to work rather than pouring more in, hoping to get faster results.

Using preventive measures to avoid clogs in the first place is the best option. You can reduce build-up by pouring boiling water down the drain and using drain screens so that debris doesn't go down the drain. For kitchen sinks, avoid dumping grease down the drain. Grease congeals when it cools, so it can easily cause clogs; it's better to collect grease in a jar or other container, which you can then either use for cooking—or even projects like soap making—or throw away.

Overall, your goal should be to reduce how much is going down your drain. Even if you have a garbage disposal, it's best to scrape your leftovers off your plate before washing your dishes, reducing the chance of clogs.

PATCHING A HOLE
IN THE WALL

Surface damage on walls is perfect for a DIY fix. Issues like electricity or plumbing can be too much for most people, but even a beginner can handle simple patch-ups. To repair a small blemish, you'll need spackle, matching paint, sandpaper, and a putty knife.

Start by clearing out any debris from the area. Use spackle and a putty knife to cover the area, and make sure the spackle is level to the wall. Next, smooth the surface with sandpaper. Generally, spackle requires 24 hours to dry, but each manufacturer will have its own instructions. Once dry, cover the area with paint, and you're good to go!

HVAC SYSTEM
MAINTENANCE

Many homeowners take HVAC (heating, ventilation, and air conditioning) systems for granted. We love what they do, but we sometimes forget they're even there; consequently, the systems are neglected, leading to stress and headaches down the road.

The Parts of Your System

Before you even try to maintain your HVAC system, it's good to get an idea of the different parts of the system. By knowing a little about each part, you'll be able to problem-solve more easily and form solid maintenance habits.

Thermostat: The thermostat is the part on your wall that controls temperature settings. It helps you determine if you want heat, cooling, or just the fan. Thermostat issues are one of the most common HVAC problems homeowners face.

Condenser unit: The condenser unit is found outside with a condenser coil on top of it. It takes air from outside and cools it using refrigerant. Blockages can lead to higher energy bills and a less efficient system.

Ductwork: Ductwork is like a road for your air to move through, often made from sheet metal or synthetic materials.

Blower motor: This part of the system forces warm or cool air where it needs to go in your home.

Heat exchanger: This device transfers heat within your HVAC system using fluids. In winter, it puts heat into your home, while in summer, it takes it out.

Evaporator coil: This part is important for cooling and uses refrigerant for cooling.

Refrigerant lines: These lines take refrigerant from the evaporator coil to the condenser coil. Leaks can cause damage and reduce overall efficiency.

Air filters: These filters collect particles from the air. Not only do they ensure indoor air quality, but they also protect the entire system from debris. Filters need to be swapped out often.

Of course, these aren't the only parts of a unit, but they are the ones you'll likely deal with most as you maintain and watch for issues with your HVAC system.

Changing the Air Filter

If you do nothing else to maintain your HVAC system, you need to change your filter. Even people who remember to change their air filters tend not to replace them as often as they should. While it may not seem like that big of a deal, the filter has a huge impact on how effectively the system performs. A clogged filter burdens the system, leading to higher energy costs and worsened HVAC health.

There's no exact amount of time you should go between filters, but based on general recommendations and your household conditions, you can get a rough idea of how often you should change your filter. One to three months is a good starting range. People with increased allergens or pets should change their filters more often. Additionally, if you use your system a lot, you'll have to change the filter more than someone who doesn't run it as often.

Changing the air filter is one of those things that you always mean to do but forget until it's been far too long. Accordingly, it helps to set a reminder on your phone or calendar for when it's time to swap that filter out. Of course, not all filters need to be changed at the same rate, so figure out how often yours needs to be replaced by paying attention to your system's needs. It's better to change them too often than too little.

Clear Debris Around the Unit

Your HVAC system, particularly its outdoor components, can be harmed by debris. Look outside for branches, leaves, or dirt around your unit, and clear it to prevent clogs. Checking often, especially after stormy weather, will prevent problems with your system. You should also clean your coils at least once a year or hire a professional. Indoor components may also be cleaned, including your supply and return registers.

Seal Windows and Stop Air Leaks

Keeping windows tightly sealed is a good way to encourage efficiency in your system. It's nice to let fresh air in — and you can still do that if that's what you enjoy — but it's important to consider that open windows may let in extra debris and pollutants. Additionally, leaks and poor seals can add unwanted strain on HVAC systems, so weather stripping and caulking are good options to seal spots that let unwanted air in.

Get HVAC Check-Ups

Just as you go to a doctor once a year for a routine check-up, it helps to schedule regular HVAC check-ups to make sure your system is still running smoothly. Most experts suggest you have your system serviced twice a year, generally just before summer and again before winter, when these systems tend to be used the most. If you live with more vulnerable people, like young kids or the elderly, these precautions are extra important.

By adding these check-ups, you can catch issues before they become more costly, so they'll save you money in the long run. Depending on where you live, these check-ups cost from $100 to $200, but they can save you hundreds of dollars by ensuring efficient energy expenditure and a longer system life.

When Going Away

Part of HVAC maintenance is planning how to handle your system when you go on vacations or trips. Making sure someone like a neighbor knows to keep an eye out for issues is a good start, but you can also take more active steps to reduce the odds of issues arriving while you're gone or when you get back.

The main step to prepare your HVAC system for a vacation is setting your thermostat at the right temperature. Some people think they should turn their HVAC systems off to save energy, but that's generally not a good idea. Instead, opt for a more energy-efficient option. These settings help you reduce energy use without risking massive strain on your system when you return. If you shut off your system completely, then switch it back to normal, it can overwork your HVAC system, potentially leading to strain and damage.

What temperature you choose will depend on your normal setting and the time of year. A good rule of thumb is to opt for a setting four degrees higher than normal in the summer and four degrees lower in the winter. In cold weather, you should never set your thermostat lower than 55 degrees because you risk issues like frozen pipes.

If your thermostat uses batteries, you may also want to swap them out before you leave. Most battery-operated thermostats need new batteries about once a year, so go ahead and switch them out if it's been about that long. Many thermostats indicate how much battery life is left, so if the indicator is low, you might as well swap them out, just to be sure your thermostat doesn't give out at the worst possible time.

CHAPTER FOUR: PERSONAL FINANCE MANAGEMENT

Building a bright financial future can feel impossible for many individuals and families. Most people understand how important managing personal finances is, yet they struggle to start the process and create habits that promote long-term financial health. While you may want an easy fix, it can take months or years to feel competent with your finances, but don't worry too much; with the right tools, you'll be going in the right direction in a snap.

CREATING A BUDGET

The first step in personal finance management is creating a budget. It may sound boring—and in many ways, it can be—but setting up a budget can be quite satisfying, and it helps you understand your spending habits better. There's no perfect way to create a budget, and what your budget looks like will depend on your lifestyle and circumstances, but there are a few tools you can use to get started.

The 50/30/20 Rule

You can use several frameworks to break down your budget, but the 50/30/20 rule is a common one. It states that 50 percent of your budget should be devoted to things you need, 30 percent to things that are nice to have but not essential, and 20 percent should go to savings.

Based on your financial situation, you may not have the funds to break things down this way, so focus first on your needs, then divide the remaining money from there. When in doubt, it's better to reduce the things in the "nice-to-have" category and maintain savings. Without savings, you'll likely accrue debt when making major purchases, so having some money set aside can save you financial woe when your washer or car breaks down.

It takes a while to build up savings, so you should reduce how much you devote to the nice-to-have category until you've saved enough to ensure that an emergency won't leave you scrambling.

Think of the 50/30/20 rule as a general guideline; not everyone will follow it exactly, but it's a division to strive for. It provides a starting point if you're struggling to use your money wisely or want to save more.

How Much Savings is Enough?

Saving money is hard for many people, but without savings, you'll end up wasting more money and struggling to cope when life's unexpected moments happen.

Generally, you want to have at least three months of living expenses saved, but six is a good target for even more security. That can seem like a lot—especially if you don't have much to spare—so don't worry if you can't reach that goal right now. Instead, slowly work toward it, and add whatever spare money you have before you spend it on something you don't need.

It helps to have a separate account for your emergency fund, so you aren't tempted to spend it on things that aren't urgent. This differentiation between savings and the rest of your money also helps you maintain a goal-oriented mindset regarding savings.

CREDIT SCORES
AND REPORTS

Your credit score plays a major role in how you spend your money and leverage debt, but many people don't know what to do about their credit scores or even what to focus on when it comes to credit.

A credit score is a three-digit number that gives creditors and other parties an idea of your "creditworthiness," which means how likely you are to repay credit. Lenders use these scores to see if you can get a loan and what interest rates you'll have. Different models are available, but the major credit bureaus give each person a credit score between 300 and 850. Generally, a score of 670 or higher is considered "good" credit.

Several factors go into your credit score, but the main one is your payment history. This part of your score ranks whether you've made payments on time. Missed payments can have a negative impact on your score for up to seven years, even if you've only missed one. Another major part of your score is how much you owe, usually based on credit utilization, which is how much of your credit you're using. If your credit cards are maxed out, your score will reflect that.

Credit scores also look at how long of a credit history you have, meaning how long you've used credit and the age of your accounts. New credit represents the portion of your score that looks at the accounts you've opened and counts hard inquiries you've made in the past year. Finally, credit mix shows whether you have a diverse credit file, including credit cards, student loans, mortgage or auto loans, and personal loans. Having diverse loans helps your score.

To improve your credit score, you must:

- Pay all bills on time and catch up on overdue expenses.
- Pay down balances on credit cards and keep credit use below 30 percent of your limit.
- Don't apply for a bunch of credit cards, as they make hard inquiries into your credit.
- Keep an eye out for fraudulent credit activity to prevent damage to your score.

No matter what your credit score is, you can likely improve it or at least take steps to maintain it. Simple steps toward improvement can make a noticeable difference if you start right now.

SAVING TOWARD GOALS

We've already talked about the importance of working savings into your budget, but it's also important to create saving goals to motivate yourself and decide how you'll spend your savings. Do you want to buy a new couch? Are you looking to make a down payment for a home? Do you want a new car? Setting goals for both the short and long term makes you more likely to save.

Investing Basics: Stocks, Bonds, and Mutual Funds

Budgeting and setting goals for savings are good ways to start improving your finances, but investing can make your money work for you. When most people think of investing, they think of high stakes plays and huge crashes. However, the true nature of investment is more nuanced, and the goal should be to make diverse and informed decisions, investing only what you can afford to lose.

When you're thinking about investment, it's good to start with small amounts of money. Not only does this ease you in, but it also allows you to hedge your bets while learning through practice. There are lots of ways you can invest. Anything that makes money from existing funds counts as an investment; thus, even putting money in the bank is investing because you gain interest in return. Different types of investments have different returns, and carefully balancing your portfolio will provide a secure financial future.

Stocks, sometimes known as "equities," are the most well-known form of investment, and they tend to offer higher risk — along with a higher payout. Stocks basically give you ownership of a portion of a company. The value of stocks changes on factors like how well a company is doing and the overall economy. When people invest too much, they stand to lose everything if the market crashes. Stocks may be dangerous for people with gambling problems because they encourage investing big to get an even bigger reward.

"Bonds," on the other hand, are investment opportunities with relatively low risk. When you buy a bond, you basically become a financial lender. Bonds are issued by both companies and governments. You get more money from what you put in because of interest from the borrower. While bonds are generally considered safer, they have differing levels of risk.

For instance, a borrower may default, and certain borrowers have lower credit ratings, causing higher risk for the lender. Meanwhile, bonds from the US government are relatively safe. Many bonds mature within five to thirty years, making them longer-term investments.

Mutual funds are another option which focus on investors using joint assets to buy securities. Portfolio managers usually handle these assets. Mutual funds can include bonds, stocks, and other cash equivalents. There are hundreds of mutual fund options, and each involves a different buy-in amount and level of risk. Mutual funds are desirable because you can buy diverse assets relatively inexpensively, allowing you to have a more diverse portfolio, which reduces risk.

The best investment for you will depend on how much risk you can afford and the time frame in which you want to receive returns. You should determine your investment strategy based on your lifestyle and income.

MANAGING DEBT

By the end of 2022, American debt reached nearly $17 trillion; of this debt, nearly $1 trillion is from credit card debt alone. Thus, debt is a common issue faced by Americans, and it can feel overwhelming to deal with unpaid credit card debts and loans. Many people feel paralyzed by debt without knowing how to start getting out of it, but with the right strategies in place, you can feel more in control of your financial future.

Step 1: Forgive Your Mistakes

Before doing anything else, you need to have some compassion for yourself. Remember that, while you may have made mistakes, you can make better decisions going forward. Forgive yourself and move on. You were likely doing the best you could at the time, and in some situations, the factors that led to debt may have been beyond your control entirely. Holding onto guilt or bitterness won't help you move forward, so it's time to act rather than wallow in the past.

Step 2: Look at Your Debt

Add up different areas in which you may be in debt to get a comprehensive understanding of your situation. These numbers can be hard to face or even cause a surge of anxiety but take a deep breath and don't panic. Now that you know what you're dealing with, you can come up with a strategy that suits your needs. Take your total income into account and reflect on budgetary needs to better understand your total financial situation.

Step 3: Choose a Payment Strategy

Now that you understand your debt, you can choose a payment strategy that helps you manage your debt. There are multiple ways to go about paying off your debt.

One method is a "debt avalanche." Start by focusing on debts with the highest interest rates and pay the minimum for the others. Keep working down in this way until all your debts are paid off. This saves you money over time by reducing your interest rates, but it can take a while to whittle debt down in this way, and you may get discouraged.

Another method is known as a "debt snowball." This strategy encourages you to start with the smallest balance, rather than the highest interest rate. Seeing those smaller debts paid off can be encouraging, which motivates you to work toward paying off larger debts. When you pay off one balance, take the minimum payment of the wiped-out debt and put that toward the highest-interest debt. This way, you're working down larger debts while experiencing wins from smaller ones.

Some people opt to focus on high credit utilization. In some cases, you may prefer to pay down the cards you use the highest percentage of your credit limit on. Credit utilization plays a major role in your credit score, so this method can improve your overall credit score as you pay debts down.

No matter which method you choose, the goal remains the same: work down debt in a way that feels doable and keeps you motivated.

Step 4: Cut Costs Elsewhere

When dealing with debt, it helps to identify areas in which you can cut costs. Things like reducing subscriptions and eating out less allow you to put that money into reducing your debt instead. You can even try to negotiate lower rates or look for more inexpensive providers. A little research and diligence can help you make the most of your money.

Step 5: Make Consistent Payments and Avoid Adding More Debt

When paying off debt, it's important to be consistent. Figure out what you can afford to pay and prioritize that payment after you've paid for primary needs. You also want to avoid adding more to your debt. Especially with credit card debt, it can be tempting to max out your spending, but in doing so, you're perpetually keeping yourself in debt instead of working your way out of it.

Step 6: Consider Debt Relief

In some cases, your debt may be so overwhelming that you just don't have the resources to manage it. Debt relief lessens the financial weight of the debt and can help you adjust the terms of your debt. The exact steps depend on the type of debt you have and how much you have.

Debt management programs allow you to work with a debt counseling agent to create a plan. These programs are helpful because they can offer waived fees and lower interest rates.

For some, bankruptcy might be the best option. Two common forms are Chapter 7 and Chapter 13. Declaring bankruptcy means you go through a legal process to erase unsecured debt (credit card bills, medical debt, or personal loans) or get a repayment plan to pay within three to five years.

You can also use debt settlement if you aren't qualified to declare bankruptcy, which means you contact your creditors or work with a debt settlement company to reduce the amount you owe.

CHAPTER FIVE:
HEALTH AND
WELLNESS TIPS

To live a happy and productive life, it's essential to know how to manage your health and wellness in a balanced and effective manner. Maintaining your health and wellness can feel like a chore, but with these tips, you can seamlessly integrate them into everyday life.

ESTABLISHING A REGULAR EXERCISE ROUTINE

Many people neglect exercise because it can feel daunting, but by making small changes, you can build your physical health, no matter where you're starting.

For many people, exercise is a must for their health. Certain physical limitations may limit what you can do, but in most cases, everyone can do some sort of exercise — and anything is better than nothing! Exercise has been proven to reduce the odds of disease and promote overall longevity; It's good for your energy levels and mental health.

Start off small. If you're not exercising at all, you can start with a few sessions a week, or even just one. From there, you can build your physical strength and abilities to ramp up your exercise routine. As with many things, the key is consistency; it's better to be consistent than to do intense activity sporadically. Even walking daily is a great way to improve your health, and it shows that you don't have to do a lot to make a difference. As you get into the habit of exercising, it will feel more normal, and you'll start to notice the change in your body and mind.

Always be realistic with your goals. If you hate running and suddenly say that you want to run two miles each day, it's probably not going to happen. Instead, opt for activities that you at least find satisfying, if not outright enjoyable. Movement shouldn't be the worst thing ever. Most people can find an activity they enjoy, so find what works for you rather than considering what you "should" do.

Try to do a variety of exercises, working every part of your body in different ways. Include cardio, strength training, and stretching to make sure your body is in overall good shape. If you're too tired for cardio one day, opt for strength training or stretching. Adapt based on how your body feels so you maintain the habit of exercising often without pushing yourself so hard that you get demotivated and give up.

If you're feeling lost about where to start on your physical health journey, attending a fitness class can give you crucial support and instruction. There are tons of fitness classes that are both highly helpful and even fun. Some classes are even targeted toward people who have little-to-no experience, so you don't have to worry about getting lost or overwhelmed.

A personal trainer is another good option. When choosing a personal trainer, consider the trainer's style and see if it aligns with what you need. Some trainers will be more encouraging and use positivity to motivate you, while others prefer tough love and harsher sessions. One training style isn't necessarily better than another, so it comes down to what you respond to.

MAINTAINING A BALANCED DIET

Maintaining a balanced diet isn't just about eating healthy; it's about finding a balance between what you love and what provides the nutrients you need. A balanced diet helps prevent disease and makes sure your body can do all the things it needs to do to reach your goals.

Colorful meals can help you maintain a balanced diet. When you eat food in a variety of colors, you're getting a range of nutrients. You also want to make sure your diet has key macronutrients: carbs, protein, and fats. Adding veggies, fruits, whole grains, and beans is also a good way to increase the nutritional value of your meals.

Be mindful of empty calories; some foods provide calories without the nutrients your body needs to survive. Foods with empty calories include highly processed foods, refined sugars, sodas or sweetened drinks, and refined grains. These foods are okay in moderation, but when you eat them, it's good to add more nutritional foods like fruits and vegetables so you're getting the vitamins and minerals you need while satisfying your appetite.

When making dietary changes, try to add things to your diet rather than subtracting them. After all, it's harder to make changes when depriving yourself of something! However, when you add the good stuff, your diet naturally becomes more balanced, and you can focus more on nutritional foods over convenience foods.

GETTING QUALITY SLEEP

Getting enough high-quality sleep is vital for your health. Research shows that people with good sleep have better moods, healthier hearts, improved blood sugar regulation, improved mental function, and less stress. Getting a good amount of sleep can transform all areas of your life because when you're well-rested, you're more likely to make good decisions.

Start a Sleep Schedule

Maintaining a sleep schedule can seem childish, but it provides a lot of benefits. Of course, there will always be moments when you can't quite stick to a schedule, but you want to go to bed and wake up at about the same time each day. Yes, that means weekends, too! Your body gets used to a schedule and thrives when you work with and not against its internal clock.

If you're a fan of napping, be careful, as naps can interfere with normal sleep. Naps should only be around 20 minutes to give you an energy boost without feeling groggy afterward. It's also better to nap earlier in the day; otherwise, you may struggle to fall asleep at bedtime, which can throw your sleep cycle into chaos.

Watch What You Eat and Drink

Before bedtime, there are certain things you won't want to have. If you've ever had caffeine shortly before bed or even just late in the afternoon, you may have noticed that it's harder to get to sleep. Even if you don't think it affects you, having caffeine too late may worsen the quality of your sleep without you even realizing it.

Other things to avoid before bed include nicotine and alcohol, which are associated with lower sleep quality and more trouble waking up.

Control Your Sleep Environment

Each person has their own preferred sleep environment, but people tend to sleep better in dark, cool, and quiet rooms. You can use blackout curtains or an eye mask if there's too much light in your room. A fan can help circulate air and keep you appropriately cool at night. Noise machines or earplugs help block out distracting or disruptive noises.

If it's been a while since you bought your mattress, you may want to invest in a new one, or at least a mattress pad, to improve your sleep quality and ensure you don't feel sore when you wake up. A new pillow may also do the trick. The best type of mattress or pillow depends on your personal preference, so consider whether you prefer a firm or soft mattress.

Reduce Bedtime Screentime

It's tempting to lie in bed and stare at your phone or other screen before bed, but it's best to go for at least 30 minutes without blue light from your screen. Blue light interrupts the production of melatonin, a hormone that helps you sleep. If you like to read before you sleep, try using an e-ink device, which is designed to be easier on the eyes. Most e-readers also have a "blue shade" or "bedtime" mode that won't disturb you like your phone or laptop.

Consult a Professional

If you're struggling to sleep, you may need to consult a healthcare professional to see if any medical causes are preventing you from getting quality sleep. Your doctor can arrange any necessary testing to identify factors disturbing your sleep and their related solutions.

STRESS MANAGEMENT TECHNIQUES

There are numerous stressors in life, ranging from work to relationships, making life difficult to handle. Luckily, having a repertoire of stress-management techniques can help you calm down and maintain a clear mindset.

Meditation

Meditation is a great way to reduce stress because it helps you learn to be present and not let your worries distract you. Online meditation tutorials and videos can help you get started and customize your meditation. For example, you can find specific meditations for work, relationships, mental health, and family.

You can also meditate just by finding a quiet place to sit. From there, focus on your breathing, and instead of trying to get rid of thoughts, concentrate on your surroundings. What are you sensing? What thoughts are in your head? When negative thoughts come up, instead of trying to avoid them, let them exist without judgment.

Utilizing Hobbies

One of the best ways to deal with stress is to turn to your hobbies. Everyone needs downtime where they can just relax and not worry about the things that are causing them stress. When you immerse yourself in hobbies for stress relief, you can revisit old interests or find new passions to enrich your life.

However, make sure you don't let your hobbies become added sources of stress. Focus on things that make you feel relaxed rather than pushing yourself to high levels of achievement. While it's good to have goals, you don't want your hobby to feel like a chore!

Seek Social Support

For many people, social support is an invaluable way to reduce stress. Being around friends and loved ones gives you a chance to decompress and vent about what is stressing you.

However, you must be careful to choose a support system that doesn't add to your stress. Find people who are willing to listen or just create a fun distraction. Calling a friend, scheduling a movie night, or going out are all good options for spending time with the ones you love.

Reduce Stressors

There will be times when there isn't much you can do about the stressors in your life. You'll feel like you have to just suck it up and deal with it. Remember, much of the time, you can change your situation, even if it feels like there's little you can do to make positive changes.

For instance, if you're struggling in a relationship, you can leave that relationship and move on. The same is true if other areas, like your career, leave you stressed. While leaving a job can be hard, it allows you to look for a new job that better fits your wants and needs. Even if you can't change the big things in life, there may be areas where you can make smaller changes.

PRIORITIZING MENTAL HEALTH

While you may be able to maintain your mental health using the tips we've provided, some people struggle occasionally or have mental health disorders that require extra help. There's nothing wrong with needing or wanting extra support. Even if you don't think you have a mental illness, seeking professional help can offer a safe place to process what's happening in your life, as well as create an action plan to help you reach goals, change negative behaviors, and discover what makes you happy.

Many people don't realize the massive effect that mental health has on their overall well-being. Mental health is a part of your overall health, after all, so don't neglect it! Poor mental health not only makes you feel bad, but it can lead to physical issues, including sleep disturbances, high blood pressure, heart problems, fatigue, muscle aches, headaches, and more.

Just as you would go to a doctor if something were physically wrong with you, the same should be true if you're experiencing mental difficulties. Everyone knows what it's like to struggle with physical health, even if it's just a common cold, and while not everything requires medical assistance, persistent or intense issues should always be checked out.

The same is true of mental health. Whether you've been struggling for a while or something just feels "off," now's a good time to reach out to a professional. A range of mental health professionals can provide support based on your specific needs.

Most people start with a counselor or therapist. These professionals focus on different methods, particularly talk therapy, which helps you talk through your issues. There are also other professionals, like psychiatrists, who generally prescribe medicine. Medication is commonly used in conjunction with therapy or if therapy alone isn't getting adequate results.

Different methods and styles achieve different results, and what you need will depend on your personality, history, and issues. Because of this, you may need to work with a few different professionals before finding something that works for you.

Research can help reduce the time you spend finding the right fit. Even after research, it may take a while to find the right professional; a big part of your relationship with a mental health professional relies on compatibility. A five-star rated professional may be great, but if they aren't great for you, you should find someone who is. With online therapy becoming increasingly popular, you have more options and don't have to limit your search based on location.

During your research, make sure the professional you choose is licensed to practice where you live and pay attention to their specialization. While professionals are trained to deal with a range of issues, they often focus on specific conditions or scenarios, just as a cardiologist has general medical training but focuses on the heart. Look to see that the professional has expertise in the area where you're struggling.

Some professionals have special qualifications to work with certain age ranges, religions, races, or other background factors. You should verify all this with the office before you book an appointment to be sure you aren't wasting your time. Most offices will answer these questions in an initial call or inquiry email.

Getting mental health care is a major step, but it's nothing to be ashamed of. It's quite liberating to address any issues you may have and create a path toward healing and improved benefits. Mental health care isn't about just talking through your issues; it's also about learning skills you can use to conquer challenges, skills not commonly taught in school.

CHAPTER SIX: SOCIAL ETIQUETTE

One of the most challenging but rewarding parts of life is social interaction. While some social skills may come naturally, others may require more practice. Even those who feel confident about their social etiquette and communication skills can improve to check in with their relationships and create even more meaningful ones.

If you struggle in social situations, don't worry; by focusing on five key areas of social development, you can empower yourself to handle any social situation with practiced ease. Social situations offer opportunity, connection, and enjoyment, and it's time to embrace these to the fullest through communication, relationship development, and conflict-resolution skills.

EFFECTIVE COMMUNICATION

Effective communication is important for any relationship, from work and acquaintances to family and friendships. Quality communication is all about using language effectively and learning to express yourself in ways that others understand. It also requires learning to listen actively and use what you hear to communicate better. By learning to listen and speak with precision and care, you can prevent misunderstandings and improve existing relationships.

Before learning anything else, you need to understand active listening. This involves listening attentively to another person, rather than thinking about what you'll say next or interrupting. Pay attention to both verbal and non-verbal cues to gain a fuller understanding of what the other person is saying. Avoid distractions and lend your full attention to the person. If you speak, do so to ask for clarification, only offering feedback to show you're interested.

Active listening shows that you respect the person talking and are willing to hear them out. It doesn't necessarily mean that you agree, but you should practice withholding judgment until you really understand another person's perspective. Think of it like mindful listening. By staying present and mindful, you can prevent unnecessary conflict and enjoy a genuine conversation. Eventually, you'll have a chance to say what's on your mind, but until then, listen actively rather than just hearing what another person is saying without absorbing it.

Now that you know the importance of active listening, you can combine that with speaking skills. To connect with an audience, you need to use concise language. While it can be tempting to employ jargon and lengthy explanations, if people can't understand, it doesn't matter how well-spoken you are or how good your point is.

The best communicators know their audience and adapt their speech accordingly. By listening first, you gain a good sense of what matters to others and how they see the world, making it easier to tailor your communication.

Remember, communication isn't just about what you say; it includes non-verbal cues and body language, which make up a significant part of our communication. If you notice someone starting to look uncomfortable, it can be an indication that your language isn't coming off as you intended. You can then adjust your speech to reflect others' responses. You won't always know what a person is thinking just by looking at them, but non-verbal cues give valuable insights into how others are feeling.

Communication requires practice. You'll become more comfortable as you practice listening and choosing your words wisely to reach your audience. Force yourself to engage in situations that require communication to develop more effective communication skills.

Navigating Social Situations with Confidence

You aren't alone if you get nervous or anxious in social settings. Millions of people have social anxiety and even those who don't sometimes feel apprehensive about certain social situations. No matter where you're starting, it's time to learn to navigate social situations with confidence.

Don't Be Afraid to Get out There

Most situations won't be as scary as you think, so you might as well get out there and practice. As you expose yourself to what makes you feel less confident, your low social self-esteem will be replaced gradually with social confidence.

Use Mindfulness

Social situations are yet another area where mindfulness comes in handy. Pay attention to how you feel, making an effort to be present in the moment and in tune with your senses. Is your heart racing? Are your hands clammy or shaky? Are you starting to feel like you'd rather be at home? These thoughts can help you understand your mental and physiological responses, making it easier to focus on the good in a situation rather than the anxiety of it.

Lean on a Friend

When in doubt, it can help to bring a friend with you to social situations while you're still getting used to them. A friend can offer much-needed support. You won't need to have a friend around forever but having their support while practicing your social confidence can give you the courage you need to put yourself out there.

Pay Attention to Others

In some situations, you may not be the nervous one, and in these cases, it helps to pay attention to others' body language. Are they fidgety? Do they seem distracted? If the answer is "yes," they may be feeling uncomfortable or anxious. Navigating social settings requires you to navigate the experiences of others as well.

ETIQUETTE FOR VARIOUS SETTINGS

Social etiquette is constantly evolving and is highly dependent on whatever setting you're in. However, gaining a basic understanding of social etiquette can give you a clearer idea of how to navigate most situations, even those outside your comfort zone. Generally speaking, the more formal the setting, the stricter the adherence to etiquette. Work functions and formal events demand a higher standard than a casual party at a bar with friends, so understanding the setting is crucial if you don't want to stand out for all the wrong reasons.

Get There Early

If you're going to an event, it's usually good to show up a bit early so you aren't rushing in at the last minute. Some events require you to arrive even earlier, such as a wedding or surprise party. No one wants to follow the bride down the aisle or come in after everyone yells, "Surprise!"

Put Your Phone Away

While you may be able to get away with having your phone out around your friends, the best practice is to keep your phone and other devices put away as much as possible; phone use impairs social opportunities and makes it seem like you aren't interested in what is happening around you.

Be Considerate of Others

The main rules of etiquette apply to being considerate of others. It makes sense that you shouldn't scream in a library or play music without headphones in a museum. If something could bother people around you, it's impolite—so just don't! You want to show respect to the people around you.

BUILDING & MAINTAINING RELATIONSHIPS

Adult friendships and other relationships can be a challenge; opportunities to meet new people seem to shrink once you graduate and enter the workplace. It can also be hard to maintain relationships you already have. All too quickly, loneliness can creep in and take over your life.

As things like your career, romantic relationships, and building a family take more time, it can feel like you have no time for your friends. It's not easy to give your relationships the attention they need to thrive, but by being a little creative, you can find solutions that fit your lifestyle. While many of these tips are designed specifically to help with platonic relationships, they apply to family and romantic relationships as well.

Forget Rejection

One of the main barriers to making new friends as an adult—or even reconnecting with old friends—is the fear of rejection. It's scary to put yourself out there! You may worry that someone won't like you or won't want to spend time with you. Try going into social situations with the expectation that other people will like you. If you don't believe it, spend fifteen minutes looking in the mirror and tell yourself, "I am likable, and people I want in my life will appreciate me." It may feel silly, but we promise it'll help.

Join Clubs and Hobby Groups

If you're struggling to find ways to meet new people, joining clubs or hobby groups is a great way to find others with shared interests. These groups are perfect because you already have common ground, so it's easy to start conversations and make lasting connections. No matter what interests you, there's a group you can join. In-person groups tend to be the best, but many people also have success with online groups, so it's up to you to decide which type of group works best for you.

You don't want to just show up to a group once, though. Be consistent in your involvement and try to participate actively. This improves your chances of building lasting connections, and people can get to know you more easily.

Make an Effort

It may seem obvious, but to make friends, you must make an effort. This means you have to initiate friendships — you can't assume that people will come to you. Sure, people may introduce themselves and try to be your friend, but why wait when you can just take the plunge?

This effort also extends to maintaining relationships; you want to show your friends that you're trying and value their friendship. No one wants to feel like an afterthought, so show how much they mean to you through action. Arrange get-togethers or suggest new ways you can connect. No one person in any relationship should be putting in all the work, so put some effort in, and you'll get something back.

Don't Expect Relationships to Be the Same

Comparing relationships is one of the best ways to ruin a friendship before it's even established. When trying to meet new friends, there's no need to compare them to old ones. Each person is unique, and it's easy to appreciate that distinctiveness if you're open to it. However, if your expectations are rigid, you'll miss out on a chance to expand your horizons.

This comparison game applies to current friends as well. People evolve as they go through different stages of life, so just because a friend was a certain way as a teenager doesn't mean they'll be the same when they're married with a baby on the way. If you're open to how your friends change and grow, your existing relationships will be more likely to endure.

RESOLVING CONFLICT

There will always be moments when you and another person simply can't agree on something. Conflict and difficult conversations are the last things many people want to deal with, but learning to deal with these things is an essential life skill.

Pause Before Responding

Practice pausing before you speak. When you take time to reflect, allowing the logical part of your brain to take over, you'll be more likely to make wise decisions, rather than ones fueled by a knee-jerk reaction. Counting to five, or even ten, before responding can give you enough time to stop yourself from saying something you'll regret.

Engage in Listening and Speaking Skills

Remember those listening and speaking skills we talked about? You need to use them whenever you deal with conflict; make sure you balance your voice with those of others.

Use your understanding to use de-escalation techniques like:

- Using a calm tone of voice and gestures to make others feel at ease rather than threatened or defensive.

- Validate others' feelings and points of view whenever possible to show that you value their opinions and respect them as individuals.
- Be inquisitive about people's thought processes, but don't use judgmental language.
- Use "I" instead of "you" — this language makes you sound less accusatory, while still allowing you to share your perspective.
- Don't let your ego stand in the way. Conflict management should be a collaborative process, not a game, where someone wins or loses. Both parties should win, at least to some degree.
- Give options on how the situation can be solved and welcome the other person's suggestions as well.
- Work with other people, rather than against them.
- Take a break if things get too intense. If a weapon is ever brought out or a physical altercation begins, realize that the situation is out of your control. Distance yourself and get to safety so you can call for help.

You may not be able to diffuse every situation, but by using these techniques and strategies, you can learn to better understand others, employing de-escalation techniques accordingly.

Avoid Defensiveness

It can be tempting to go on the defensive but remind yourself to take some deep breaths. It's important to gain a clearer understanding of any situation before jumping to conclusions or feeling attacked.

Some ways to avoid becoming defensive include:

- Ask questions to clarify what a person's statement or actions may have meant and use active listening. It's too easy to misunderstand and get defensive because of our own insecurities. Most people are not intentionally malicious.
- Accept any responsibility you may have for a conflict but acknowledge that your role doesn't mean you're a bad person. Mistakes aren't the end of the world and don't doom you to a terrible fate.
- When you receive criticism, consider whether it's constructive. Most people mean well but don't always know how to say what they're thinking. If it's not helpful, the other person may be lashing out because of their own negative feelings, rather than meaning to hurt you specifically.
- Take deep breaths as needed to ride the waves of tension.
- Remind yourself that your emotions cannot control you if you stay aware of them rather than ignoring them.

These techniques will help you manage situations that bring out intense feelings and prevent escalations — at least on your end.

Choose Compassion over Passion

There's nothing wrong with being passionate, but it's common for people to get so fanatical about what they believe is right that they lose compassion for the other people involved. Remember that no matter what, we're all human.

This doesn't mean you should excuse toxic behavior or accept mistreatment, but you must understand that people are complex, and each person deserves respect. When you choose to have empathy, you stop seeing others as obstacles and start seeing them as real people.

Maintain Non-Threatening Body Language

When dealing with a tense situation, the last thing you want to do is make another person feel threatened because of your stance or body language. Always respect others' personal space. Don't loom over them or get in their face. Try to look calm and collected instead of showing anger. If someone feels threatened, they'll instinctually react to the perceived threat, becoming defensive, which can make it almost impossible to reach a positive conclusion.

Don't Assume People Are Rational

As much as we like to think that we are reasonable beings, sometimes, people simply aren't rational. Consequently, you should never assume someone is using their head over their heart. In conflict, we often say things that don't make logical sense and may not even be consistent. If you assume someone is acting rationally, you risk sounding condescending or speaking in ways that make them feel attacked.

Consider Deeper Issues

In many conflicts, there are deeper issues at play. At an office, someone taking the last donut may not seem like that much of an issue, but to the person who missed out on it and is mad about it, that donut may represent something bigger in their life. Maybe they feel like they always run just short of getting good things. People are bothered by many different things, and by recognizing that many conflicts have deeper issues, you'll start to learn how to overcome those challenges.

It's Not a Zero-Sum Game

When some people experience conflict, they get to a point where they may want to win for the sake of winning and see any compromise as losing. In life, most things aren't a zero-sum game. A win for you doesn't have to mean a loss for another person, and vice versa. When you diffuse a conflict, you've both won because you've chosen to work through your issues rather than letting them fester.

Find a Resolution Through Common Ground

Most people can find some kind of common ground, and this is a great place to find a resolution; it shows that you both share something bigger than yourself. Common ground is a great way to form bonds, even when other factors tear people apart. Shared interests or beliefs connect you, allowing you to meet in the middle.

If Needed, Find a Mediator

Sometimes, you and another person simply cannot work your differences out on your own. In these cases, it may be a wise idea to get a mediator of some kind. It's best to find the most neutral party available, who you know will be fair and allow everyone to offer their side of the story. Mediators can offer much-needed advice and help everyone calm down. They can often give suggestions for compromise, too.

CHAPTER SEVEN: TIME MANAGEMENT

No matter who you are, you only have 24 hours each day. If you're like most people, it likely seems as if you never have enough time for work, play, and basic needs such as eating healthy and sleeping.

There's no way to make your days any longer, but you can learn to maximize your time by using time management and productivity techniques. Whether you want to create goals and to-do lists, manage and avoid distractions, or simply find a reasonable work-life balance, the goal is to find more time for what makes you happy without neglecting your responsibilities.

DEFINING GOALS & PRIORITIES

If you want to be more productive, you need to have goals. Goals form a roadmap that gives you direction, so you don't wander aimlessly, wasting your time and worrying that you'll never gain the satisfaction you crave. No matter which area of life you want to improve, goals can help you stay focused and boost your motivation when things get hard.

Creating an Effective To-Do List

On paper, making a to-do list seems like the easiest thing in the world, but not all lists are created equally. Understanding how to make an effective to-do list will help you expand your already-done list. Creating a to-do list will keep you organized, making sure none of your priorities slip between the cracks.

There are different ways to create a to-do list. You may choose to write it in your daily planner or schedule. This is a simple way to organize tasks that you need to get done each day. While you can use a digital medium to keep up, research suggests that physically writing information down helps you retain it, so writing out what you want to get done helps you remember.

You can take this step further and use the "1-2-3" task method. This method involves organizing your tasks into three lists: The first includes your time-sensitive tasks, the second includes important but not pressing tasks, and the third focuses on unimportant tasks you can do if you have extra time. Prioritizing your to-do list can help you get a better sense of what you should do first and what can wait.

You can use three different columns for this method or try other techniques, such as using only one list but highlighting tasks in different colors based on priority. In fact, breaking out your favorite office and art supplies is a great way to get you excited about this otherwise-tiresome activity. While the 1-2-3 method has proven to be effective, don't be afraid to get creative and explore different styles of creating to-do lists!

Overcoming Procrastination: Tips for Getting Things Done

Procrastination is an all-too-common—and unhealthy—coping mechanism that many people turn to. While it's sometimes mistaken for laziness, procrastination is just a way to avoid the negative feelings and pressure that come from certain tasks. While procrastinating can alleviate stress in the moment, it often causes even more anxiety in the long run. Fortunately, by adapting your mindset, you can learn to live a life free of procrastination.

Be Honest with Yourself

Before procrastination destroys your productivity, you must be honest with yourself about why you're putting something off. At first, you may not be able to figure it out, but introspection can help you get to the bottom of it.

What are you afraid of? Why does the thought of completing a project make you so nervous? Is the task overwhelming you? Do you feel you can't handle certain sections of the assignment? A mental block exists for every procrastinator, and some digging will allow you to determine what your wall is so you can create an entry to more productive thinking.

The Sky Isn't Falling

You may be familiar with what's sometimes called the "chicken little effect," which is the tendency for little things to send your thoughts spiraling, causing you to feel like the sky is falling despite everything being fine. As a result, you become paralyzed by your anxiety, afraid to do anything because of that persistent fear that it could all go wrong.

When you find yourself thinking in this way, pause and ask yourself if the terrible outcome you fear is realistic. Yes, perhaps the worst-case scenario could come true, but the chances of that are usually slim. Remind yourself that, in most situations, even when things don't go according to plan, you can problem-solve and learn to overcome hardships.

Focus on Long-Term Consequences and Rewards

At times, procrastination may be caused by short-term wants or rewards. You want instant gratification, so you work on tasks you can get done right away while the bigger tasks are neglected. Think about what actions will give you long-term satisfaction.

Pull Out Your To-Do List

Remember how we talked about the value of a to-do list? Well, to-do lists are a great tools to put off procrastination (see what we did there?) Use your list to keep yourself on track and stay mindful of what you need to do. As a bonus, you'll be encouraged as you check items off your list.

Be Goal-Oriented

Always keep your goals in mind as a driving force for your behaviors. When you find yourself procrastinating, think of your goals and remind yourself that you need to take action to reach them.

Set Reasonable Expectations

Lots of people procrastinate because they've set unrealistic goals for themselves. If you try to complete a five-day task in two hours, you're setting yourself up for failure. Give yourself enough time and resources to avoid getting stressed about running out of juice before you've even started. If someone else tries to set unrealistic goals for you, communicate that and reach a solution that's more realistic based on your needs and abilities.

Be Mindful of Your Work Environment

If your work environment is full of distractions and stress, you'll likely be more prone to procrastination. Adjust whatever parts of your environment you can to create a calming, organized workspace.

Find an Accountability Buddy

Reaching out to another person who struggles with procrastination can help hold both of you accountable when all you want to do is make excuses about why you keep putting something off. You can challenge each other's thinking and analyze the real reasons for your procrastination together.

Praise Yourself When You Succeed

Procrastinators tend to not give themselves the praise they deserve because their anxiety has created a cycle of delayed responsibilities. Even once a task is completed, they don't always feel the satisfaction they crave because of stress and the reduced quality of a rush job.

When you reach a goal, take a moment to appreciate your accomplishment—no matter how small—rather than rushing on to the next task. By doing this, you feel more competent and less like an impostor.

Let Go of Perfection

Many procrastinators are also perfectionists—the reason they put off a task in the first place was that they fear it won't reach their high standards. They can become so afraid of failure that they're unable to complete tasks, ironically causing them to be more likely to fail.

You're only human, so let go of perfection, and instead, focus on doing your best work. Even if you make a mistake, it most likely won't be the end of the world. After all, mistakes are opportunities to learn and grow, so being "perfect" isn't all it's cracked up to be.

MANAGING DISTRACTIONS

There are many reasons why you may not be as productive as you want to be, but one of the top reasons is that you're distracted. Maybe you've got a lot going on at home, or you're worried about all the parts of your life you can't control. Maybe there's simply a place you'd rather be. Whatever the distraction, learning to focus on the task at hand is an invaluable tool for being more productive.

Some ways to manage distractions include:

- Using Do-Not-Disturb mode or other focus modes.
- Limit your notifications so you get only what you need.
- Schedule specific times to check your email—preferably during times when you're less productive, such as early morning or right after lunch—and don't look at it outside of those times.
- Keep your inbox clear and organized to avoid losing important emails in a pile of spam.
- Keep off social media and personal messaging unless something urgent comes up, even when you're simply trying to focus on a hobby.

- Reduce distractions in your environment, using tools like earplugs, noise-canceling headphones, or anything that helps limit sensory overload.
- Stay organized so you always know what task you're doing and don't feel like you're aimlessly wandering through your day.
- Set boundaries with other people and politely let them know if you'd like them to give you time and space to focus.
- Know your temptations and avoid them.
- Take care of your physical and emotional needs, such as staying hydrated, being well-rested, and scheduling regular, short breaks to take care of these needs or recollect yourself.

These suggestions are just a sample of steps you can take to improve your focus. If you have other tools that work for you, add those in as well. You'll likely need to experiment to see optimal results, so pick one thing to try first and incorporate others as you progress.

FINDING A WORK-LIFE BALANCE

One key to productivity is maintaining a work-life balance. Without it, you can experience burnout, fatigue, increased stress, and an overall lack of well-being. Finding balance requires practice and attention, but it's something anyone can do.

Set Boundaries

If you're trying to find a balance between work and the rest of your life, the first thing you need to do is set boundaries. This may mean that you don't answer work emails outside of business hours or you don't answer personal texts during your workday. The goal is to create a clear distinction between work and pleasure so you can focus on whatever you need to do at that particular time.

To create these boundaries, you may need to have serious discussions with your boss, coworkers, clients, family members, or friends to ensure your boundaries are being respected.

Commit Your Full Attention

When you're at work, you're at work, and when you're at home, you're at home. If you're spending time with your kids or partner, don't check your work email constantly. Likewise, you shouldn't constantly check in with your family or friends while you're at work. Use the boundaries you've created to commit your full attention to whatever you're doing, rather than dividing your attention, which will only lead to poor performance in all areas. Of course, there will be times when you'll be distracted, but do your best to focus on the task at hand.

Not Every Day Has to Be Equal

Many people think balance means having an even split between different areas of their lives, or that they should devote a certain amount of time to each thing each day, but that isn't strictly true. Balance is about finding a good relationship between different areas in your life that's sustainable in the long term.

Some days, you may have to work longer hours and not have as much time for your family, or you may take off an entire week to go on a family trip. Balance isn't as simple as a fraction—life is so much more dynamic than that! The key is learning to adapt to circumstances and find balance accordingly.

Make Concrete Plans

If certain parts of your life feel out of balance, plan to spend more time on what you're lacking. Don't just say that you "should do" something; instead, work concrete plans into your schedule to hold yourself accountable, and don't keep putting off tasks that will bring you the work-life harmony you need. When you have specific plans, it's easier to maintain boundaries with yourself, coworkers, and loved ones.

Don't Be Afraid to Take Time Off

Everyone needs time off, for a range of reasons. Whether there's been a death in the family or you're feeling mentally or physically under the weather, taking time off doesn't mean you aren't a dedicated employee or worker. By taking time off, you allow yourself to recharge, and you'll be better at your job when you return.

Define Yourself Fully

People often lose a sense of balance when they create a sense of self by depending too heavily on single parts of their lives. For example, someone may define their success solely on how well they're doing at work, which can lead to reduced satisfaction in other parts of their lives. Then, when something goes wrong at work, it feels even more devastating because there's nothing to balance it out.

You're never just one thing. You aren't just an employee, partner, friend, or anything else; you're a composite of all the roles you fill in life.

CHAPTER EIGHT: TRAVEL PLANNING

If you're looking to add adventure, knowledge, and global awareness to your life, traveling is a great way to experience new things and challenge your perception of the world by embracing other cultures. However, for many people, travel can cause stress and anxiety, leading to the feeling that travel is more effort than it's worth.

The key to stress-free travel is learning to be smart, arming yourself with insider tips on how to upgrade your plans. From deciding where to go to staying safe and healthy, this chapter is your concise guide to traveling like a pro!

RESEARCHING DESTINATIONS & BOOKING FLIGHTS

The first thing you want to do is research. Decide where you want to go and what methods of travel will get you there safely and cost-effectively. Think about when you want to go based on what you want to do at a certain destination. For instance, you might not want to go to a destination during its rainy season, or in the summer, when it's miserably hot.

Spend some time learning about your possible destinations, including any cultural differences they may have. When you do your research, you're less likely to get in over your head or be caught unawares, and you can prepare for different situations that may arise during your travels.

PACKING ESSENTIALS

While it's normal to want to make sure you pack a lot, so you don't forget anything you need, packing light allows you to travel smarter, with less clutter taking up your mental and physical energy.

The first rule to packing light is to bring what you know you'll need and not things you might need. Chances are, if you find out you need something you don't have, you'll be able to find it at your destination without much problem, so think about the essentials of your trip and only pack those.

Beyond packing only the essentials, you should also consider how versatile items are. Items with multiple uses that you can mix, and match gives you a lot of utility without weighing your luggage down. If you can only use a certain item for a singular purpose or moment, you may want to think twice about bringing it, unless that item is essential for something specific.

If you're going on a longer trip, packing a week's worth of clothes is advisable for anyone who wants to pack light. While you may not look forward to doing laundry, committing to it can drastically reduce how much you have in your luggage, and it doesn't really eat up that much time.

For those new to packing light, a trial run can help you ensure there are no gaps. Try living from the items in your suitcase for a week and see what works well and what isn't as useful as you might've thought. Starting to pack well in advance allows you to explore your options and make better choices.

NAVIGATING AIRPORTS & SECURITY CHECKS

Airports can be an absolute nightmare, especially unfamiliar ones. However, armed with information, you'll get through airports and security checks with minimal stress.

Each airline and airport has its own guidelines and standards, and if you're traveling internationally, there may be even more regulations to adhere to. Thus, it's crucial to research airlines and airports thoroughly. Checking out their FAQ pages is a good starting point, and most clearly outlines their regulations so passengers are never going in blind. This includes getting a general sense of the layout of the airport and where you'll need to be.

Additional steps you can take to prepare include:

- Wear shoes that are comfortable and easy to remove.
- Don't wear anything metallic on your clothes or accessories.
- Make sure liquids in your carry-on are three ounces or less and packed in a quart-sized, clear bag.
- Pack so that, if your bag needs to be checked, things can be easily removed for inspection.
- Double-check the banned item list while packing—then check it again before you leave.
- Before getting in the security line, make sure your ID and boarding pass are handy.
- Remember to remain calm and be polite, carefully following any instructions you're given.

- Arrive a couple of hours before your flight boards to avoid having to rush, giving yourself plenty of time to adapt to any unexpected situations that might arise.

Navigating through an airport can be a challenge, but when you walk in knowing you're prepared, you can breathe a sigh of relief and start your trip off on the right foot.

EXPLORING TRANSPORTATION OPTIONS

Travel is all about getting from place to place, so determining the right type of transportation for you will help you maximize your time and fulfill your priorities. What works for one person may not be ideal for you, so consider your circumstances and what you feel most comfortable with.

Public Transit

If you're on a budget, it's hard to beat public transportation. Yeah, you might have to deal with crowds and hectic schedules, but public transit is good for both the environment and your wallet. Some places have better public transit systems than others, so researching your options before you go is essential.

Rental Cars

If you want to be empowered to travel on your own terms, rental cars are an ideal option, allowing you to move from place to place and make your own schedule. However, rental cars can be expensive, and certain areas may be stressful to drive through or have unfamiliar traffic laws, so this might not be the best option for some people.

Ridesharing Services and Taxis

If you don't want to deal with driving yourself or public transportation, ridesharing or taxis might be the best option for you. These options can get quite expensive, so many travelers like to use them in moderation and only when a quick, reliable form of transportation is desperately needed. Use caution when taking advantage of these services; make sure any taxis are valid and official, and only use rideshares from legitimate companies.

Walking, Bikes, and Beyond

If you want to be more active on your trip, walking or biking can get you from place to place while keeping you mobile. These are often fun ways to experience places more fully as you go from destination to destination. Of course, these methods require more work, but they're affordable, sustainable, and can add an extra layer of adventure to any experience.

Staying Safe and Healthy While Traveling: Tips for a Smooth Trip

Being safe and healthy is a top priority for all travelers, so keep the following tips in mind to promote safety for yourself, your group, and everyone around you.

- Don't carry too many valuables with you and limit displaying things like expensive jewelry.

- Be careful when drinking; you want to remain sharp and aware of your surroundings.
- Make sure you have multiple payment methods, and keep them in different places; that way, if you lose one, you won't be stranded without resources.
- If you're going abroad, register with your country's embassy and have their contact information handy. It's also a good idea to supplement your health insurance with a travel plan in case of medical emergencies, as most plans aren't accepted outside the country.
- Verify your lodging reservations (hotel, bed & breakfast, etc.) before you arrive at each destination.
- Always have enough money to cover unexpected emergencies or living costs, especially if you're going abroad.
- Pay attention to your surroundings.
- For important documents, keep copies in case they get lost or stolen.
- Use reputable companies for things like transportation and lodging.
- Maintain regular contact with friends or family so that, if something goes wrong, the response will be faster.

Traveling can be scary—especially if you're doing it alone—but by taking a few simple steps, you can be prepared and have more peace of mind. That way, you'll spend your time enjoying your trip rather than worrying about all the what-ifs or struggling when challenges pop up.

CHAPTER NINE:
TECHNOLOGY & GADGETS

Technology is all around us, and whether you love it, hate it, or have a love-hate relationship with it, it's part of modern life. Having a certain level of tech literacy and knowing how to maintain a healthy balance with your tech life will ensure that you can maximize your time, energy, and overall sense of well-being.

BASIC COMPUTER SKILLS

Computer literacy is something many people need to have just to get by with their jobs, social life, and normal functioning, as many daily behaviors involve basic computing skills. Nevertheless, some people still feel a bit lost when trying to deal with computers. If you feel like you're behind the curve, you can catch up by learning some key terms and functions, which will make navigating the virtual world more efficient and stress-free.

Keyboard shortcuts are a great way to maneuver through computer work more quickly. These shortcuts allow you to use certain combinations of keys to perform common operations. This saves you the time it takes to search for the right command, causing fewer interruptions in your workflow.

Different computers and operating systems use slightly different shortcut keys and commands. For instance, Macs use the command key, while PCs use the control key.

Before we get started, certain keys are listed as abbreviations, both on your keyboard and the internet. Of these, the most useful to know are command (Cmd), control (Ctrl), delete (Del), function (Fn), and escape (Esc).

The keyboard combinations below use the "+" symbol to indicate that you should press both keys simultaneously. The shortcuts we've listed below are for PC, but these shortcuts can be used on Mac by swapping the control key for the command key unless otherwise specified.

Now, without further ado, some basic keyboard shortcuts include:

- Copy: Ctrl + C
- Cut: Ctrl + X
- Paste: Ctrl + V
- Undo: Ctrl + Z
- Re-do: Ctrl + Y (Shift+Cmd+Z on Mac)
- Select All: Ctrl + A
- Print: Ctrl + P
- Find in document/page: Ctrl + F
- Save document: Ctrl + S
- Italicize/remove italics: Ctrl + I
- Bold/remove bold: Ctrl + B
- Underline/remove underline: Ctrl + U
- Close current document: Ctrl + W
- Open a new document: Ctrl + N
- Add link: Ctrl + K

These are just a sample of useful shortcuts, but you can easily look up others online. Researching your specific needs can help you find niche shortcuts that may not be as common but could be useful for your purposes.

USING SMARTPHONES AND APPS

Smartphones put a lot of power in your pocket, and this functionality can enhance several areas of your life, including work, personal, and social. The following tips are designed to reduce digital clutter and help you make the most of your apps.

Organize Your Home Screen

There's no perfect way to organize your home screen, but by considering what you want to get out of your phone, you can organize your home screen in the most convenient way for you. For instance, the apps you use most frequently should be easily accessible, while those you use less can be organized into folders or even kept off your home screen altogether.

While it can be tempting to use your home screen for everything, sticking to what you use the most reduces clutter, ensuring you can always find what you're looking for. Most smartphones also have a search feature you can use instead of having to sift through tons of apps.

Be Choosy About Notifications

Before opting into notifications, think about whether it's really helpful. Only set up notifications for things that are important. Silence other notifications so you don't get overwhelmed or distracted by constant alerts from your phone.

You can also apply "focus" settings that allow only certain notifications to come through, like "Do Not Disturb" and

"Airplane" mode. For instance, while you may want to make sure you're notified of work emails during the day, you may want to shut those notifications off when trying to relax at home.

Embrace the Cloud

"Cloud storage" allows you to upload information so you can retrieve it from anywhere. This type of storage may seem intimidating and potentially risky, but it helps you access your files across devices, frees up disk space, and helps you avoid major issues if your hard drive fails.

Of course, you should be mindful of what you're putting on the cloud, but as long as you're careful and take steps to keep your cloud secure (such as by using multi-factor authentication), you can achieve great results by embracing cloud storage.

Limit Screen Time

If you're struggling to balance your smartphone use — especially when it comes to social media apps — you can go into your settings and place limits on how much you use certain apps. These limits will give you a warning when you've hit your predetermined limit so you're mindful of how much time you're spending in certain apps, allowing you to limit yourself in whatever way provides the balance you need to live a more productive life.

Improve Battery Life

Keep an eye on the battery life of your phone or other devices. Certain activities take more power, so while you're using these features, you may want to reduce screen brightness or disable other features to preserve battery life. GPS, Bluetooth, and videos all use a lot of power. If you need to use these features often, carrying a portable charger is a good idea.

INTERNET SAFETY & PRIVACY

The internet is a magnificent resource, but it's also full of dangers that you should be aware of to protect your digital identity and real-life safety. From identity theft and data breaches to phishing scams and phony emails, there are tons of ways malignant actors can take advantage of you as you use the internet. These general safety guidelines are not only good for you, but they are parameters you may want to share with your family and friends.

Use a Secure Internet Connection and VPN

While you may want to go somewhere with public Wi-Fi, like a coffee shop or café, you're more vulnerable when you're using a public network rather than a secure internet connection. If you choose to use a public network, getting a VPN, or "virtual private network," is a good way to protect your data because it encrypts the data you send on a network. VPNs can offer additional protection, not just on a public network, but for anyone who wants to protect their privacy more effectively.

Add Extra Password Protection

Having a strong password is necessary for every account, especially those containing personal information. Don't use the same password across accounts, though; if you do, once a cybercriminal cracks that one password, they'll have access to multiple accounts. Passwords should be at least 12 letters long, containing a mix of upper and lowercase letters, numbers, and symbols. Using a password manager can help you create secure passwords and access them easily, with no memorization required.

It's also advisable to have multi-factor authentication, which requires you to have at least two verification techniques. One of these techniques is usually a password plus another method, including answering security questions, a one-time password sent to your email or mobile device, biometric identification like fingerprint or face recognition, or an authentication code.

Multi-factor authentication protects you when your password fails, so it's especially important as scam artists continue to improve their effectiveness at breaching personal data.

Make Sure Websites are Reliable and Legitimate

When visiting a new website, use caution and look for signs that it is what it says it is. If you see a lot of grammar errors or low-quality images, proceed with caution. Additionally, inconsistent website themes or odd payment options may suggest that something isn't right.

Using third-party services can also reduce your risks. For example, PayPal is a good option for online purchases; it provides additional coverage, ensuring you don't give potentially risky sellers your credit card information directly.

It's always better to be safe than sorry. If something doesn't feel right, don't give a website the benefit of the doubt—close out that tab! Often, a quick online search can help you determine whether a website is legitimate or just another scam.

Don't Click on Links

If you see a link in an email, if there's any chance it's spam, go to the website directly by typing the address in rather than using the link. For instance, if an email tells you a transfer didn't go through and you need to "click here" to fix the issue, instead, use your web browser to sign into your account and verify if there's really a problem.

Download with Caution

Many cybercriminals put malware in downloads, which offers them a backdoor to your sensitive information. Malware can be disguised in apps or other downloadable files, so make sure you're downloading from reputable sources and check for a website's trustworthiness before blindly believing a file is safe.

Use Social Media with Caution

Social media is a great way to connect with people and share your interests, activities, and life experiences. However, you need to think about who might be seeing your posts and how someone might misuse your content. When posting, don't share too much identifying information, such as your location, social security number, or date of birth.

It's also helpful to make your accounts private when possible and monitor who's following you. Once information is out there, it can be impossible to prevent unintended uses, so always think carefully before posting.

When meeting people online, always assume they may not be who they say they are. The internet and social media are great ways to meet people who share your interests, but cybercriminals often pose as someone who shares your interests to exploit you. Be cautious with your online relationships, just as you would for in-person meetups.

Fact-Check

As nice as it would be to just search for something and get the right answer, it's vital to double-check what you read. Misinformation and disinformation can easily creep into your media and obscure the truth. Check that the websites you use have reliable sources, and if something seems untrue or skewed, check other sources to see if you can verify it.

While disinformation is intentional, misinformation is often an unwitting process of people spreading fake information they don't realize is false. Both types of wrongful information are dangerous, so fact-check thoroughly — and encourage your friends and family to do the same.

TROUBLESHOOTING COMMON ISSUES

When something goes wrong with technology, it can cause a huge inconvenience. It quickly becomes frustrating when you don't know how to troubleshoot your issues and get back to business as normal. Cut down the time you spend getting upset at your technology by learning to manage some of the most common issues.

When in Doubt, Turn It Off

It seems almost comedic that the first step to any tech problem is usually turning something off and back on again. When dealing with technology, sometimes problems can cause chain reactions that lead to your device refusing to cooperate. By restarting, you begin with a clean slate, perhaps solving the problem altogether.

Make Sure You're Up to Date

If you notice that your software isn't running the way you want it to, you should check to see if there's an update available. Sometimes, issues can only be resolved with an update. You can also try uninstalling and reinstalling software if your problems persist. It's also good to check for updates on your hardware.

Reset for Relief

Resetting is often an extreme step, but most devices can be reset to their factory or default settings, which can fix a range of issues. Unfortunately, taking this step usually erases all your data and preferences, so you'll want to back up any important files before you do this. Only reset if you've exhausted all other options and are prepared to lose your data.

Make Sure Cables Aren't Loose

When a device stops working or doesn't seem to be charging how it should, stay calm; these sorts of problems are commonly caused by a loose cable. Before you panic, check all cables, making sure they're firmly connected at both ends. Especially when you have a lot of cables, they can easily wiggle out of place just enough to cause trouble.

Tech Support is Your Friend

When you've exhausted the extent of your technical knowledge, there's nothing wrong with reaching out to tech support. It may take a little time, but tech support can help you pinpoint a problem by relying on trained parties who have a clear process to help you troubleshoot.

Keeping Up with the Latest Tech Innovations

You likely don't need to be a tech expert, but it's always a good idea to keep up with emerging trends, as these can drastically impact how you interact with the world around you and handle work tasks. Adding some tech news outlets to your routine can give you key insights without becoming overwhelming. Committing to learning and evolving with technology helps ensure you never fall behind with new developments that can benefit you.

CHAPTER TEN: CAREER DEVELOPMENT

Whether you're firmly established in your career or are just getting started, navigating career development and personal growth can feel burdensome. Whatever your situation, you can put your best foot forward in your desired profession by learning about the job you want, networking with professionals in your field, negotiating salary and benefits, and continuing your development for prolonged success.

WRITING A WINNING RESUME

The goal of a résumé is to highlight what makes you stand out to potential employers in a concise manner. Having a strong resume can help you snag your dream job by showcasing the best parts of yourself.

Use the following tips to make a résumé that stands out:

- Start with a template to organize your resume.
- Unless you're in a specialty area or have gaps in your resume, put your most recent work at the top and list items chronologically.
- Make sure your name and contact information are eye-catching and easy to find.
- Add a summary at the top of your resume providing a brief snapshot of who you are and why you're the perfect fit for the job, and tailor it to fit the specific job you're applying for.
- Use succinct language.

- Choose action verbs like oversee, analyze, or generate, rather than phrases like "responsible for," when highlighting your achievements.
- If applicable, use numerical figures to highlight your achievements.
- List only relevant career history, rather than every position you've ever held, unless you're just starting out.
- Emphasize unique features that make you stand out.
- If you have certifications, list them.

MASTERING THE JOB INTERVIEW

When it comes to job interviews, your answers to questions can be the deciding factor between getting the job and losing it to another candidate. No matter how qualified you are, if you don't do well in the interview, you likely won't get the job.

Tell Me About Yourself

When an employer asks you to tell them about yourself, offer a concise statement about what makes you an ideal fit for the position and how your unique skills and attributes set you apart from other candidates.

Why Would You Like to Work Here?

It's easy to answer this question generically, but it's better to research the company to show how your goals and values align. Showing a potential employer that you're knowledgeable about their specific company shows how interested and diligent you are.

What Are Your Strengths and Weaknesses?

It can be hard to identify strengths — and uncomfortable to examine weaknesses — but when asked this question, always opt for honesty rather than what you think they want to hear. For strengths, give specific examples of where you shine and how these qualities have proven useful in your career.

On the other hand, when discussing weakness, focus on areas that are difficult for you, and explain — succinctly — how you're working to improve in these areas. You can even highlight how the position can help you improve your weak areas. For both, storytelling is a great way to illustrate your point.

Where Do You See Yourself in the Future?

Interviewers often want to know where you see yourself in the future. For this question, you want to paint a vibrant picture of the future you see for yourself. Show your passion and ambition but try to keep it relevant to the job and how this job fits into your plan.

Talk About a Time When...

It's common for potential employees to be asked about past experiences or hypothetical situations they might run into. In both cases, it's important to give concrete examples of what you've done or would do. Use your storytelling skills to show how you would respond to challenging situations.

Asking Your Own Questions

During an interview, don't be afraid to be inquisitive and ask about the company. Your answers should highlight what you're looking for in a work environment and show that you're passionate and active. Employers like potential employees to show excitement about the position, and asking questions helps you show your energy.

NETWORKING LIKE A PRO

For anyone looking to improve their career, networking is an important tool to create valuable connections that you can use to improve your prospects and meet people who've had similar career experiences. Networking allows you to make friendships, establish mentorships, and create partnerships that can last years or even decades.

If you want to start networking, the best way to start is by finding where other professionals in your industry are. These can include online spaces, but in-person spaces like conventions or seminars are ideal. In this way, you can expand your circle and get to know people who may help you improve your career and create new opportunities.

The key to networking is that you can't be shy! You must be ready, not only to put yourself out there but to listen actively and be inquisitive; people will respond more positively if they think you're interested in them. Additionally, when networking, you want to make long-term connections, so following up with people you've met and gradually building your relationship is important.

Networking isn't easy for everyone, but it's pretty straightforward. If you're nervous, just start by saying, "Hi!" and introducing yourself. It can help to have business cards with your contact information at hand.

NEGOTIATING SALARY & BENEFITS

Whether you're looking for a new job or trying to improve conditions at your current job, negotiating benefits is a vital skill. Without it, you may end up getting paid less than you deserve and lacking the benefits you may want or need. Many employers are willing to negotiate—all you have to do is show them why you deserve more and how investing in you will benefit them.

Talking about salary and benefits can be anxiety-inducing, and you may be tempted to accept whatever you can get. If you're excited about a job opportunity but it has downsides—a long commute, lacking benefits, or low pay—you can take steps to balance that with better pay and benefits.

Highlight these factors and explain how they should influence how you're compensated and be sure to mention how having you as an employee benefits them, whether because you've been in the industry a long time or possess a wide skillset. You can also mention your education, career level, or geographic location to show why you might be due more money. Look at comparable salaries in your area to see what you can generally expect.

Once you've thought about what you have to offer and why you deserve more benefits, make your case. Create a marketing campaign for yourself, highlighting the skills and attributes that make you valuable. With these points in place, schedule a time to discuss benefits and have a respectful conversation. You might feel some tension, but if you're confident and willing to compromise, you can negotiate something that works for both of you.

CONTINUING EDUCATION

While you may think that once you have all the required degrees you can finish your education and focus on your ordinary workload, that isn't always the case. Ambitious people know that to get the results they want they must continue learning and developing their skills.

Sometimes, this may mean earning a higher degree or certification in a specific area, but it can also mean more informal skill development, including seminars, online courses, podcasts, books, or journals. It doesn't always matter how you continue your learning, but the goal is to set yourself up for future success by expanding your mind and honing your skills.

CHAPTER ELEVEN: OUTDOOR SURVIVAL SKILLS

Some people love outdoor adventures, while others would prefer to stay inside as much as possible. Whether you love the great outdoors or not, it's important to have some idea of how to survive should anything bad happen or if you just feel like challenging yourself to an outdoor adventure.

BUILDING A SHELTER

There's no getting around it; humans need shelter. If you ever find yourself stranded, you'll want to know how to create a safe and relatively comfortable shelter. In a dangerous situation, building a shelter protects you from the elements — and may even save your life.

The first step is choosing a suitable location with enough space. Ideally, find a place with a water source nearby, such as a river or stream, so you can easily get drinking water, but stay about 200 feet away to avoid contamination. Beware of spots with natural hazards like wildlife or places that are likely to flood or have landslides. A flat location with a sight slope is a good choice. You also want to look for natural items that can add protection, such as caves, trees, or rock formations.

When you've found a location, note what resources you have around you. Depending on the climate, you'll need different items. For example, in a cold climate, you want items that are insulating, while in a rainy climate, you'll need to protect yourself from getting wet.

Start to imagine how you can use these resources. Brush, like twigs or dead branches, are usually easy to find and require less effort than having to remove living branches. Leaves and grass are also readily available in many locations. When using items like rocks or other heavy materials, be wary of how you lift them, so you don't injure yourself.

With your materials gathered, start building a frame for your shelter with longer branches, making sure they're sturdy. If you can, lean these materials against large rocks or trees to add stability to your structure. Create a dome or triangle, and once you get your "poles" in place, secure them to the ground with logs or rocks and tie them together. Reinforce as needed with additional poles.

Next, add insulation, covering the poles with it. Materials like leaves, grass, and bark all work well for insulation. Remember to leave gaps for ventilation so you can breathe in the shelter. In warmer environments, you want protection, but not so much that you feel like you're in an oven!

With the insulation in place, create a sloping roof for your shelter by adding and securing poles to the top. Flexible materials like vines can help secure the roof poles and give them the needed slope. If needed, you can add more insulation to the outside of the shelter to improve waterproofing.

Building a shelter isn't easy, so if you really want to test yourself, try spending an afternoon in nature and see if you can build one for yourself.

FINDING FOOD
& WATER SOURCES

If you're ever stranded in the wilderness, you'll need food and water. Before you do anything else, find water because you can survive longer without food than water. The good news is that you'll most likely find groundwater or running water. When you find a source of water, see if nearby wildlife drinks from it; if they do, you likely can drink it, too.

However, you don't want to drink the water straight from the source. Always purify it first by boiling it. If the water is cloudy, use a cloth, towel, or coffee filter to filter the water. Sand, gravel, and certain plants can also be used in a pinch.

Now that you've got water to drink, it's time to think about food. It's important to only eat things you recognize, though, so as not to accidentally poison yourself! Some items that are easily identifiable and safe to eat include cattail, dandelion, clovers, amaranth, and burdock. You can also try catching fish and other wild animals.

Things like berries and mushrooms can be a good choice, but only if you're well versed on which ones are safe to eat and which are poisonous. When in doubt, it's better to be cautious; humans can survive days or even weeks without food, so you make sure you're eating something safe.

NAVIGATING WITH A MAP & COMPASS

Using a map and compass is relatively easy, but it's a skill many people simply don't have these days. However, when you're in the wilderness, these tools can help you find your way in the great outdoors.

Study your map, giving yourself time to understand it, and look for landmarks to help you navigate more easily. This will help you better orient yourself, especially if you don't have a compass.

If you do have a compass, begin by checking its calibration by making sure the north needle and red arrow are aligned. When using the compass, place it flat on the palm of your hand. If you're also using a map, place the compass and the map on a flat surface for increased accuracy. Then, look for where the travel arrow aligns with the degree dial to figure out which direction you're facing. Using this degree, you can find yourself on the map and move in the appropriate direction.

STARTING A FIRE

If you want to stay alive in an emergency scenario, you've got to know how to start a fire. Fire keeps you warm and allows you to cook and prepare safe drinking water.

To start a fire, find a spot away from low-hanging branches, debris, brush, and other potential hazards. Choose a location with a good amount of dry wood around you. Most campsites have established firepits or rings — but of course, in survival settings, that probably won't be the case. In dry locations, you must be especially cautious.

If you don't have a firepit or ring, look for a flat space. If you can't find a suitably flat spot, you'll want to build a mound fire. Use soil, gravel, or sand to create a mound that's three to five inches thick to contain your fire. You want the mound to be wider than the size of the fire you plan to build.

You'll need a fire starter, which can include a lighter, matches, or flint. It's always good to carry these items with you if you're going to be in the wilderness. Having multiple methods available is good in case one doesn't work.

Then, look for wood from dead trees whenever possible, making sure it's dry; green or wet wood won't burn as easily. Small and dry materials can serve as tinder, including wood shavings, cattail fluff, dry moss, pieces of paper, or dry bark. You'll also need kindling, which is the next-largest layer — things like twigs, sticks, or chunks of bark.

Finally, you'll need larger logs to create a lasting fire. Logs don't necessarily have to be huge, and small logs actually burn better when you first start the fire, but you'll need to add logs more often if they're small.

With your wood collected, begin building the structure of your fire. Among the most common is a "lean-to" fire, a versatile formation that stands up well to wind. To create this fire, place a large log upwind in your fire pit and lean smaller logs against that log. In addition to helping block wind, this larger log provides a built-in cooking surface. Make sure to leave gaps so you can access the area and allow air to flow.

Next, bundle your tinder and lean it against the larger log, underneath the others to shelter it from the wind. You can then add your kindling around the tinder. Add larger-diameter kindling, putting them against the large log. You can then light the bundle of tinder. Add smaller logs as they burn, leaning them against the larger log, to keep the fire burning.

STAYING SAFE IN THE WILDERNESS

When you're in the wilderness, you're bound to run into some wildlife. When this happens, the most important thing is not to panic. Most animals won't hurt you, but certain creatures do have the potential to cause problems.

Always keep your distance from wildlife whenever possible. Remain vigilant so you don't wander where you shouldn't go. If there's a chance you'll face dangerous animals, you want to be prepared; whenever you go to a new place, research what animals might be there and how to respond to an attack, as each animal is different.

For example, when encountering bears, the general rule is, "If it's black, fight back; if it's brown, lie down. If it's white, say goodnight." Obviously, none of these options are great, so the best policy is to avoid trouble with wildlife by keeping your distance and staying aware of your surroundings in the first place!

CHAPTER TWELVE: PERSONAL GROWTH & MINDSET

In life, it can be all too easy to get stuck. You feel like you're doing the same thing every day, and your life starts to lose meaning because you feel like a passive party in your own story. Fortunately, by developing a growth mindset, you can keep challenging yourself to grow and maintain a sense of purpose and self-development.

CULTIVATING A POSITIVE MINDSET

Having a positive mindset is the best way to keep yourself on track for success. Maintaining a positive mindset allows you to focus on what you can do rather than wasting time worrying about all the things you can't do. In this way, you remain an active force in your own future instead of feeling like things are always happening to you.

To develop a positive mindset, try the following:

- Pay attention to your strengths and remember them when you struggle.
- Look to your goals as a motivating force to remind you of why you want to keep going.
- Show kindness to others.
- When negativity creeps in, shift your focus to positive things.
- Practice self-care techniques to calm down and find peace.
- Be more compassionate toward yourself.
- Always remember your higher power—that thing that reminds you that life is bigger and more meaningful.

- See the good in others, and you'll see the good in yourself more easily.
- Make a list of things you're grateful for and what you're excited to experience each morning.

Negative thoughts sometimes function as a defense mechanism — you may think that if you prepare for the worst, you won't get disappointed or hurt when something bad happens. However, holding on to negative thoughts drives you away from your purpose and all the things you can do to influence your destiny. You can't always keep bad things from happening, but you can control your mindset as you come up against obstacles.

SETTING & ACHIEVING GOALS

We've already talked about the value of goals and how to set them in other sections, but now, it's time to dig a little deeper and understand how to use these goals to promote personal growth.

A commonly used method for setting goals is the "SMART" goal method designed by George T. Doran (1981). If you've ever learned anything about setting goals, you've probably heard this acronym before, but if you haven't, it stands for: Specific, Measurable, Achievable, Relevant, and Time-bound.

Now that you know what the letters in "SMART" mean, let's break it down further by discussing what, exactly, this entails:

Specific: Specific goals are clear and understandable. They explain precisely what you want to accomplish. By being specific, you don't end up feeling lost. Vague goals can get confusing and, thus, demotivating.

Measurable: You must have some way to measure your progress. For example, you may want to improve an area by 80 percent. If you don't have a way to measure your goal, it's hard to tell whether you're making progress or not.

Achievable: While it's good to dream big, some goals simply aren't realistic. Make sure your goals outline things you can realistically achieve. For instance, setting a goal to build a mansion in a day is unrealistic. Lofty goals get overwhelming, so you're likely to quit before you even get started.

Relevant: Your goals should apply to what you want to accomplish in life. Setting goals that align with your values and desires will keep them relevant. Never set a goal just because it's what you think you should do, or because you want to accomplish something.

Time-Bound: All goals need some sort of deadline. Setting a scheduled endpoint keeps you motivated, making it more likely you'll follow through. You can adjust the deadline as needed, but having an idea of when you want something done ensures you're proactive and don't put off working toward your goal.

When making SMART goals, you can also use incremental goals, which means breaking larger goals into smaller ones. Incremental goals help you monitor your progress and provide positive feedback, making you more likely to stick with it. A good foundation for your goals will help you turn dreams into reality.

BUILDING CONFIDENCE

Experiencing self-doubt is common, but it isn't usually constructive. By learning to overcome these negative feelings, you can be confident about who you are and what you can do.

Eliminate Negative Loops

Many of the negative thoughts that cause self-doubt stem from "negative loops." Negative loops often come from past experiences or messages we've internalized. For example, a child whose bullies tell them they are stupid may have a negative loop in which their internal voice repeats: "You're stupid." If you've got a negative loop in your head insisting you aren't good enough, it's time to push back against those thoughts. Consider why you're nervous and what you fear might happen. Acknowledge the fear, and you can work to change it.

Don't Compare Yourself to Others

One of the best ways to promote confidence is to stop comparing yourself to others. People are so different that, if you get so focused on what other people have that you don't, you'll never appreciate what makes you unique.

Be Around People Who Lift You Up

The people you surround yourself with have a profound impact on your confidence, so choose to spend time with people who lift you up instead of those who drag you down. Pay attention to the people who make you feel good about yourself. If you notice yourself feeling bad about yourself around someone, create stricter boundaries with them or stop associating with them beyond what is required.

Fake It Until You Make It

Confidence requires practice, so while you might not feel more confident right away, faking it can eventually create real confidence. When you enter a room, stand tall and walk with your head held high; when you start acting like you believe in yourself, you'll begin to feel more capable and in charge of your mindset.

Embracing Failure

Failure isn't a fun part of life, but it doesn't have to be debilitating. It's common to associate failure with a lack of competence or think it means something is inherently wrong with you, but in most cases, that's simply not true. Think of failure like data. When you fail, it gives you information you can use to improve next time.

Learning from failure is a key part of survival; if we didn't learn from failure, we'd keep making the same mistakes. There's a reason that "trial and error" is a common phrase! Every mistake offers the chance to do better next time and improve yourself, so make failure a productive part of your life.

PRACTICING GRATITUDE & MINDFULNESS

When life feels hard or you feel like you aren't making any progress, practicing mindfulness and gratitude can help you manage challenges with grace and find inner peace in any situation. Juggling everything isn't always easy, but with the right tools, you can find happiness in everyday life.

Gratitude is the practice of being thankful for what you have, rather than worrying about all the things that seem to be spiraling out of control in your life. This practice helps you focus on the good and find hope and resilience when times are hard.

Mindfulness means paying attention to your senses and remaining in the present moment. Rather than thinking about all the things that have gone—or might go—wrong, pay attention to your current surroundings, allowing yourself to act with more clarity and not based on your worries or past hurts.

Gratitude and mindfulness work as a team, granting you the ability to appreciate and be present in every moment. When you can do this, you'll feel more at ease within yourself and have the confidence and calmness to deal with any situation.

CONCLUSION

There's no way to learn how to do literally everything in just one book, but the goal of this book is to teach you the fundamental life skills you need so that, no matter your situation, you have a foundation and the tools you need to figure out how to do everything else.

You're now empowered to problem-solve and do things you may have been intimidated to try before. Rather than having to outsource, you can be more autonomous and confident in your ability to handle any situation. Life is full of unexpected moments, and though you never know what may be ahead of you, you can rest assured, knowing that you're ready to handle each situation better.

Reviewing What You Know

This book has covered a lot, so if you don't feel like you're quite there yet with all the skills, don't worry. You can always return to the chapters in this book to brush up on a certain skill or review a tool when you need it. Because this book is a lot like a toolbox, you can come back to it for support and guidance whenever you feel unsure or unable to handle your responsibilities.

Practice Makes Perfect

From basic life hacks to meaningful relationships and fulfilling careers, this book covers all areas of your life, allowing you to find balance in whatever makes you feel the most fulfilled and at ease. The most important step you can take now is to practice the skills you've learned.

While there are some quick and easy hacks in this book, most of what we've covered requires practice. For instance, if you don't have prior experience, you won't just be able to pick up a knife and cut food perfectly right away. Likewise, if you're struggling to progress in your chosen career, it can take months to get back on track and feel good about your job. Fortunately, no matter how big your goals or life changes, by taking little steps forward, you can manage big, overwhelming journeys with relative ease.

Don't wait to put these lessons into practice! It's easy to keep putting off change until tomorrow but challenge yourself to change your life right now before it passes you by and you wonder why you didn't try to improve yourself sooner.

Sharing Your Skills

If you think you're the only one who feels a little lost in life, know that everyone feels that way sometimes, and it's common for people to be anxious about their lack of skills, especially if they feel like they are behind their peers. There's no shame in not knowing certain things—life is hectic and nuanced, so there's always room for improvement, even in areas where you excel. Take a deep breath and commit to gaining more knowledge, rather than focusing on what you don't know or are still learning.

Likely, other people in your life could benefit from learning these skills, so if you see a loved one struggling, sharing how you've applied the lessons in this book can help them make meaningful changes in their own lives. You may even want to make changes with someone you love, such as a friend or partner, and in doing so, you can motivate and help each other to hone your skills and self-development.

Finding Peace for Yourself

Ultimately, we hope this book helps you find peace — along with the balance and confidence you need to succeed in every part of life. Continue with the lessons you've learned by customizing these skills and tools for your purposes, striving to grow and develop continuously as a person.

Life is full of challenges, many of which can feel overwhelming and scary, but there are very few things you cannot overcome with an attitude of growth and resilience. Now, get out there and take control of your future!